BUILDING BETTER LEARNERS

The Snapp Approach

EDITED BY

Dr. Darlene H. Schmidt

Order this book online at www.trafford.com
or email orders@trafford.com

Most Trafford titles are also available at major online book retailers.

Printed in the United States of America.

ISBN: 978-1-4669-1212-0 (sc)
ISBN: 978-1-4669-1522-0 (hc)
ISBN: 978-1-4669-1523-7 (e)

Library of Congress Control Number: 2012902864

Trafford rev. 05/19/2012

 www.trafford.com

North America & international
toll-free: 1 888 232 4444 (USA & Canada)
phone: 250 383 6864 ♦ fax: 812 355 4082

CONTENTS

Dedication ix
    Learning Begins at Conception ix

Acknowledgements xi

Disclaimer xvii

Preface xix

Edward A. Snapp, Jr. And CCDE Background xxiii

Memories Of Ed Snapp xxix

Introduction 1
    Genetic Memory 2
    Milestones for Motor Skills 4
    Sensory-Motor Development 5
    Chronologically Controlled Developmental
    Education (CCDE) 7
    References 9

SNAPP CCDE Principles 11
    Introduction 11
    SNAPP CCDE Principles (Chronologically Controlled
    Developmental Education) 12
    SNAPP's Dimensions 14
    The Three-Finger Salute 15
    References 19

Foundation of Movement 20
    Human Learning 20
    About the Environment 22
    Sensations and Movement Patterns 24
        A. Flexion Positioning 25
        B. Surface Sensations 27
        C. Deep Pressure Stimulation 36
        D. Flexion 43

   E. Extension...47
   F. Rotation and Sequencing of Arms and Legs 52
   G. Crawling...59
   H. Creeping 69
   I. Walking 70
   References...72

Visual Perception 73
   Ed Snapp in the Classroom...73
   Visual Information..74
   Procedure for Perceptual Development..............................75
     Activities: Contrasting Dark and Light 75
     Open Palm Tracing for Visual Development..................80
     Ball Tracking Activities...86
     Eye-Hand Tracking..91
     Comprehension and Recall Abilities 92
     Visual Perceptions Tips 101
   Read the Following Books: 104
   Reference 104

Chronology of Reading, Writing, and Spelling 105
   Factors Relating to Reading and Writing.......................105
   Examples of Varied Learning Activities 109
   Language Comprehension 110
   Fact Teaching...113
   Reading SNAPP Silhouette Cards 115
   Reading Sequence...120
   Handwriting Sequence..133
   Spelling..141
   References...148

Chronology of Math...149
   Math Chronology..149
   Recognition and Identification 151
   Addition 167
   Subtraction..176
   Conclusion 184
   References...186

Synopsis of *Building Better Learners* 187

Chapter References 191

Glossary—CCDE Definitions 194

APPENDIX A: SNAPP's Dimensions 203

Appendix B: SNAPP Cards 207
    Making the Cards 207
    SNAPPing the Cards 213
    Reading the SNAPPed Card 217

Appendix C: Deep Pressure 218

Appendix D: SNAPP Writing Instrument 219
    Materials Needed 219
    Instructions for Construction 220
    Child's Position for Writing 223
    Grasping and Loading the Instrument 223

DEDICATION

This book is dedicated to the memory of Ed Snapp and to the preservation of his innovative educational methods.

Learning Begins at Conception and Continues Throughout Life. Ed Snapp

Ed Snapp, a physical therapist, was always in a learning mode and designed an educational program when seeking an answer to, "When does learning begin?" Snapp called his educational program Chronologically Controlled Developmental Education (CCDE). This program reinforces and/or recaptures abilities of the nervous system that are remembered and stored as memories within our Genetic Code. *Building Better Learners* is evidence of this legacy. *Building Better Learners* explains the importance of the Genetic Code sequencing of sensory-motor learning and the importance of the proper environments associated with this sequencing.

The original environment of human development is in the Mother's womb. This environment is wonderfully prepared for the baby and is the place where he initially learns. He sequentially learns the reflexes of flexion, adduction, inward rotation, and their release; he then learns pre-natal extension, abduction, outward rotation, and their release. Learning and retaining these sensory-movements in their genetically coded **proper** environment and in their **proper** sequence is the Key to Excellence of the Genetic Code.

After birth the proper environment for immediately learning to integrate these prenatally learned reflexes into coordinated movement is a warm, quiet, distraction free room with dimming light controls and a firm, slick surface on which a baby can easily move. Again, sequentially learning to use these developmental movements in an associated environment is crucial to Unlocking Excellence.

CCDE replication of the prenatal environment, where initiation of movement originally occurs, includes: warmth, darkness, fluid, a beanbag chair or inner tube to hold one in a prenatal position, and the rhythmic heartbeat sound. CCDE replication of the neonatal environment where learning and or relearning to use prenatal movements occurs is a warm, quiet, distraction free room with dimming light controls and a firm, slick surface on which a child can easily move.

It is genetically coded in our development that prenatal and neonatal movements integrate into a higher level of coordinated movements that lead to crawling. Crawling, as explained in *Building Better Learners*, allows the baby to learn to coordinate the use of his shoulders, arms, and hands with his hips, legs, and feet. After integrating these movements he will connect his vision to the use of his hands. This new coordination allows the baby to expand his world and his learning abilities by movement and vision.

According to Ed Snapp, P. T., there is a sequential order as to when new learning abilities should be initiated. For example, mobility patterns advance from the Basic Crawl to the Homolateral Crawl to the Cross Pattern Crawl to Creeping, and finally to walking. Brain processes also advance from awareness in visual perception, to reading, writing, spelling, and Math to complete understanding of these learning abilities. Advancement in mobility patterns is associated with advancement in levels of brain activity.

This program will developmentally advance your child through various levels from large movements to smaller movements, from large print to small print, from understanding concrete objects to understanding abstract concepts, and from recognizing an object to analyzing an object. The activities in this book will guide you, the parent, in working with your child to achieve a completed background with a 90% mastery level.

ACKNOWLEDGEMENTS

This book was the enthusiastic effort of seven dedicated educators who knew and loved the late Edward A. Snapp, Jr., Physical Therapist. Over the years, all have taken his courses and supported him in his efforts to help individuals and to improve instructional methods in schools. The incredible information of this book comes from Ed Snapp's courses, workshops and lectures and our various personal conversations we have had with Ed since 1975.

All have made essential contributions to this work, especially **Dr. Betty Ward** who transcribed all the DVDs provided by **Susan Snapp,** Ed Snapp's daughter. Our group would have been forever working on this project without their effort.

We give special recognition and thanks to Susan Snapp who graciously shared the collected DVDs and unpublished articles written by Ed. Susan has been instrumental in maintaining the Ed Snapp Foundation that has helped preserve the legacy of Ed's unique concepts and application of his methods to ultimately benefit all of us as well as future generations.

We extend special appreciation to **Roxanne Small**, Physical Therapist, author of *Building Babies Better* for her editing of the material. Her assistance to our endeavor has been invaluable. Roxanne began studying with Ed Snapp in 1981. We also offer our special thanks to **Julie Erbaugh**, Physical Therapist, for her efforts in the editing of the material. Julie studied and worked with Ed in his clinic. We also offer special thanks to **Lucas Haunsperger** and **Lucy Alff** for serving as models for our photographs and to **Scott Smucker** who developed the Deep Pressure illustrations.

Our journey with *Building Better Learners* began in October of 2006 and we quickly nicknamed ourselves "The Book Group". We were honored and very aware of the awesome undertaking to preserve the perceptive educational methods of Ed Snapp, the man whose thought processes could project light years backward and/or light years ahead.

Each of us had been in one or more of Ed Snapp's two-week courses and/or his weekend courses several times. We each had our numerous volumes of notes on paper and in our heads even though Ed Snapp never used one page of notes during his classes. He talked and taught and we took notes and reminded him of break time, lunchtime, and long after 5:00 time. "The Book Group" encapsulated thousands of bits of information from our notes and from our heads that Ed referred to as "just the tip of the iceberg" or "just a scratch on a mountain" of what is yet to be discovered.

"The Book Group"

Lucy (elementary and special needs teacher) successfully used SNAPP Cards in the first grade classrooms for 7 years. Also for 20 years, she helped many first, second, and third grade special needs students by including a number of the Snapp developmental exercises and the SNAPP Cards in her daily lessons.

LUCY ALFF: 2 B.S. Degrees, M.S.

Pam (physical educator, coach, classroom teacher) has been nonstop in promoting Ed Snapp's developmental methods because of her immediate improvements from doing them. She also witnessed unbelievable achievements in her students and athletes even with limited application of Snapp's methods. Most memorable from her teaching/coaching career is not the trophies and meets that were won but the abilities gained by students with disabilities who learned movements while flat on the gym floor

PAM GRIMES: B.A., M.ED., M.S.

Fill (all level teacher, coach, band director, consultant 19 years for elementary physical education at Texas Education Agency) assisted Ed in setting up CCDE workshops in several state universities; coauthored a grant request that was approved but at that time all grant funds in this area of Education (Title III) ceased before this and other educational programs could be initiated.

FILL HENDRIX: B.S., M.S.

Pati (special needs teacher) worked very closely with Ed Snapp. She was one of his clients, concentrating on visual functions for herself. As her personal problems were "fixed", she used Ed's CCDE methods with her classes of special needs children. After retiring Pati coordinated Ed's office in her locale. Pati did not see this book come to fruition. She lost a yearlong battle with cancer in 2010.

PATI MARIK: B.S.

Marcella (teacher/coordinator of Health & Physical Education) "Since Ed's first class in 1975 I have followed and wholeheartedly supported the use of Ed Snapp's methods by parents and teachers. Ed's methods are the developmental components necessary for understanding abilities and disabilities in learning and coordination. Parents should find this book helpful to improving their child's abilities."

MARCELLA PORTER: B.S., M.ED.

Betty (educator, researcher, numerous certifications) explored various methods of teaching and found that nothing was better than Snapp's CCDE methods in advancing students in their educational abilities. She is a scholar of Ed's program. She continues to read current medical and scientific research and delights in finding support of CCDE methods. It is amazing that Snapp designed his program before the availability of this modern research technology.

DR. BETTY WARD: B.M., M.ED., Ph.D.

Darlene (all level teacher, coach, college professor) "With three degrees in physical education, I thought I knew all about movement and teaching. Ed blew my mind! I began using his methods with my university team and in my age group gymnastic classes. The changes in movement patterns were truly unbelievable! What a mistake I made by not documenting the changes that I witnessed in both younger and older students."

DR. DARLENE SCHMIDT, B.S., M.A.T., Ph.D.
   Editor

We have grown in Ed Snapp's thought processes during these past years. Ed Snapp has shown us how to unlock abilities of "Excellence" that have been learned, retained and passed on by the Genetic Code. We now celebrate the completion of *Building Better Learners* and we know that we have, in our way, begun to preserve Ed Snapp's contributions to education for present and future generations.

DISCLAIMER

Medical Disclaimer: The FDA has not evaluated the statements in this book. These methods are not intended to diagnose, treat, prevent or cure any disease. The information provided by the authors and editor is not a substitute for a face-to-face consultation with a health care provider, and should not be construed as medical advice. Individual results will vary, depending on the child's physical abilities, as well as the adult's physical ability to demonstrate, apply, and provide the methods and materials as described. Parents should use good judgment about their own physical abilities when considering demonstrating any of the activities in this book. Parents should also use good judgment about the physical abilities of the child when considering the activities to be done by their child.

Use of methods and activities: The methods and activities should be used only according to instructions provided, in a manner consistent with the educational approach developed by Ed Snapp. The editor and the authors have received direct training from Ed Snapp in applying his educational methods and activities. They have reported successful outcomes for their students who received such instruction. However, there has been no formal statistical/research testing of the educational outcome for individuals who have received education via these methods and activities versus those who have not had that experience. Likewise, the ability of individuals to follow the instructions as provided in this book has not been tested.

The authors, publishers, and/or copyright holders assume no responsibility for any alleged loss or damage caused, or allegedly caused, directly or indirectly, by the use of information contained in this book. The material is not intended to replace the services of a physician or therapist.

PREFACE

In this book you will find information on how you can help your child be better equipped to successfully respond to academic instruction as well as increase his level of coordination in all activities—including sports.

Concepts of sensory-motor education are not new. Years ago researchers, working with children with learning problems, created programs that included sensory-motor activities to help improve learning. Some of these programs have been around for decades and some have been refined. Unfortunately most of the time, the programs have been used only when helping individuals who had obvious disabilities. It is the intent of the authors to preserve as much as possible the teachings of Ed Snapp who saw the potential of using these CCDE activities in elementary school classrooms to enhance the abilities of all children.

Dr. Empress Zedler (former professor at Texas State University, San Marcos, Texas) was often heard to say she learned so much from the children she was trying to help. She would give this illustration:

> One day I had an elementary school age child standing with her back to a blackboard while facing me. I asked the child, "What does 2 x 2 equal?" The girl answered that she did not know. But while she was saying this, I noticed that the child was making the numeral 4 with her right hand. Suddenly it dawned on me to turn the child around to face the blackboard and I gave her a piece of chalk. I asked the question again. The child began to answer, "I don't . . ." and she paused as she then realized her right hand was writing the answer on the board. "Four", she said.

This is a wonderful illustration showing that sometimes we must appeal to more than one of our senses in order for the child to convey the correct answer.

A new mother tells of her experience with her baby's eyes. In 1980 at Michael's one-month well-baby check up, the doctor said that Michael's eyes were not working well together; that is the eyes turned outward (wall-eyed) rather than being centered and were not able to work together. So she made an appointment with an eye specialist. The date was set for three months in the future.

Knowing that Snapp's prenatal activities created an environment in which the eyes as well as the limbs learn movements, the mother decided to put Michael in an inner tube to hold him in the prenatal position. He was in this position for 3 hours a day for the usual duration of his nap.

By the time of the appointment with the eye specialist, three months later, the doctor could find no trace of the wall-eyed condition. Had the diagnosis been wrong, or had the mother provided the right activities in the right environment for Michael's nervous system to develop appropriately? We believe it is the latter.

This material can be used successfully with all ages, including adults. We tell the following story to show differences this program can make in an adult's life. At a CCDE training workshop conducted by Ed Snapp, attended primarily by elementary education teachers and a few college professors, some attendees noticed a young elementary school teacher who appeared rather quiet and withdrawn. His eyes appeared unfocused. He even walked with his head down. Two years later he attended a second CCDE training session. He was a changed person. The changes included a difference in his eyes; now both appeared to work together. Now we saw a person who walked with his head up and with a "spring" in his step. An interesting aspect about him was his personality change; from a very quiet withdrawn person to almost the opposite. What a wonderful thing to observe! When asked what he had done, he simply replied, "I followed Mr. Snapp's program."

These are just a few of many examples we could include to help you understand how by following this text you can work to improve all areas that are involved in learning.

The material contained in this book, *Building Better Learners*, is primarily for children who would normally walk into the First or Second Grade. Children in Pre-K and Kindergarten could benefit from the activities found in the Chapter "Foundations of Movement" as well as activities found in other chapters. These activities include but are not limited to Open Palm Tracing for Visual Development, Ball Tracking Activities, Eye-Hand Tracking, Fact Teaching, Recognition of Objects, Pounding and Counting, and Matching Varied Rhythms.

For additional information on home CCDE programs read (1) *Do Butterflies Carry Spare Parts?* by Sarah Bryce, a parent who used CCDE with her son, Malcom and (2) *Different: The Boy Who Couldn't Write* by Margie Boyd, a parent who also used Snapp's methods with her son, David.

For parents or professionals interested in using Snapp's teachings with a younger child, such as an infant and toddler, see the book *Building Babies Better* **by Roxanne Small, PT.**

EDWARD A. SNAPP, JR. AND CCDE BACKGROUND

This book has been written especially for parents. It is about some of the methods and techniques of Edward A. Snapp, Jr., an extraordinary physical therapist who was a leading pioneer in the area of innovative physical therapy and innovative ways of presenting academic content.

Ed Snapp was born June 29, 1925, and grew up in Houston, Texas. Before he graduated from high school Ed was training as a competitive swimmer and had hoped to sometime compete in the Olympic Games. Upon graduating from high school, he enlisted into the United States Army Air Corps. He had hoped to become a pilot and fly a Lockheed P-38 Lightning. Another of his plans was to prepare for a career as a physician. But those plans would not happen, for early one morning Ed awakened with a fever and headache that became progressively worse during the day. A spinal tap at the hospital indicated meningococcal meningitis and he became comatose for several days. Upon awakening he could not move except for the weak movements of his left fingers and toes. He could breathe and talk. The diagnosis now included acute anterior poliomyelitis. All his plans went out the window.

After a few weeks of therapy he was told that he might be able to walk again with braces and crutches. This did not set well with the 18 year old Snapp. With his great determination, he was out of the hospital and home in a short time. In about 10 months he had gradually improved to the point of being able to take a few careful steps.

Ed's father, E. A. Snapp, Sr., a physical educator, literally carried Ed to the swimming pool at the YMCA five days a week. Within a few days Ed could make it across the pool in about the same time he used to swim 200 yards. It felt good. Swimming was the closest thing he had to independence. Because of the constant care of his father who gave Ed daily therapeutic massages, he was able to walk again.

Because of his experience with polio, Snapp was asked, as a volunteer, to talk to kids about exercises for polio. He was concerned that he might give some wrong information, so he inquired about enrolling in physical therapy classes at the University of Texas Medical School in Galveston.

He applied formally but was told that he could not be a student there because physical therapy was limited to females only. In a short time though, a letter came from the Galveston UT Medical School. He told his mother to throw it away. Fortunately she opened and read it. It was a letter of acceptance.

His formal education was completed after physical therapy school. He later took specialized courses, such as those dealing with brain injury. He worked in the physical therapy department of Hermann Hospital in Houston. It was his intention to do physical therapy for about six months and then teach swimming, his first love.

The Harris County Polio Treatment Center in Houston had heard of Snapp's volunteer work with children with polio. He was offered the position as head of its Physical Therapy department. He accepted the position.

A major polio epidemic occurred from 1948 to 1950. During this time, Snapp saw about 3,000 cases of acute polio at the hospital, in his private practice, and at the Polio Treatment Center. His 18-20 hour workday proved to be too much for his afflicted body, so he left the Polio Center. Doctors had told him to quit one or the other; either his private practice or his work at the Polio Treatment Center; he chose private practice.

Private practice seemed the best approach. He designed his own equipment that he needed because it was not available elsewhere. He had several patients, each needing a new method of improved equipment. The equipment he designed did not take up much space, was adjustable, and could accomplish what he was not able to do otherwise.

Dr. Paul Harrington, a genius surgeon, was in charge of orthopedics at the Hermann Hospital. He had developed an internal fixation for spinal injuries. Snapp and Dr. Harrington worked closely together and eventually a 14-inch rod was inserted in Snapp's back that made life much better for him.

Ed worked with many clients with Cerebral Palsy but was concerned that his clients were not getting good results. He reasoned that it was because the Physical Therapy (PT) prescription was inadequate. Invariably it read: "PT 1 hour for 2-3 times a week" or something similar. According to current practice, what Ed was doing was appropriate but he pushed for treatment five times a week because he thought it would be more effective.

Some of Snapp's clients walked so well in the clinic setting that strangers thought that the clients did not actually have cerebral palsy. But that was inside the clinic. Once they were away from the clinic, they walked as if they had had no treatment at all. Ed realized that what he was doing was teaching them a skill—they could walk better while thinking about walking, but outside the clinic they were distracted, so they reverted to their old way of walking. It was obvious to Snapp that teaching them the skill of walking correctly did not did not carry over to real life.

In his private practice Snapp educated therapists in precision work that was unusual at that time. While these therapists remained working in his private clinic, he was able to leave the clinic for two or three months a year to visit different clinics and specialists all over the country. This was practical education for him, for he learned something at every location—even if it was things not to do.

This practical education gave him a broad insight of techniques before moving into his specializations. He attended conventions dedicated to handicapped children. He spoke with well-respected neurologists of that time including some at the Institute for Human Development in Philadelphia. One of the ideas had to do with the background development of all creatures throughout historical times as well as children's development. This group had started working with children by having them crawl like infants (on the tummy).

In working with techniques from the Institute, Ed realized that it wasn't a specific exercise that improved some of his clients. He thought possibly that the achieved improvement at the Institute was because the nervous system was trying to "fix it". That was a correct assumption! The problem was how to get back to that earlier time period to allow the nervous system to "to fix it".

One new patient—a five-year old girl with cerebral palsy—had been in physical therapy for four years prior to meeting Ed. She had made no improvement in her movement patterns. At her home Ed sat her on his lap and held her in the prenatal position to see if it would do anything for her. He began to feel her arms relax. She seemed to enjoy being in this position. Fascinated with her reaction, he put oil on their kitchen table and placed her hand on it and moved her hand around. She began to move her hand on her own. He thought, "Boy, if everything would be that easy!" Later she was walking properly and using her hand. Eureka! Is this the way to get the nervous system back to an earlier time period?

His main problem was how to take the nervous system back to an earlier time period. Could going back to the prenatal time period help? If so, how? Would the environments of the prenatal position and a firm, slick surface help?

Ed really did not understand anything about prenatal time. He talked with some medical doctors and asked, "If I put them (children) into a prenatal fetal position and turn out the light, and so forth, and they decide they are in a prenatal situation, will they quit breathing?" The doctors wouldn't even talk to Ed about this. The child psychologists, when asked the same question, were "in unison" with the doctors. They did not know!

But Ed was convinced—he had to know. He reasoned ". . . a lot of people place themselves in this position and sleep in the dark and wake up in the morning still healthy. So it probably is safe." Even so, the first time Ed put a child on his side on a bed, propped things all around so as to make him feel encased, and turned off the lights - - - he said, "I guarantee you I was this far away . . . listening to him breathe!" Remarkably, some of his clients began to make rather quick changes. Of course he appreciated that, but realized that it was not his doing, but the nervous system fixing itself, at just that level.

He kept thinking about what other things could happen in the prenatal environment. What about the mother's heart beat? He asked a doctor to make an audiotape of what was going on inside the mother's womb. That did not go over well with the doctor. The next year a doctor in Japan did exactly that—Ed had missed his chance to become a multimillionaire!

He realized that the more he was able to duplicate the prenatal environment the better the nervous system worked in correcting its own problems. Ed began to arrange a sequence of activities from prenatal environment through the newborn process of basic crawling—innate patterns that are learned by all humans.

He studied embryology. Everyone starts out as one cell. The cell divides into two cells, etc., proceeding from globular cells to a flat plate, which rolls up into a "taco" shape. Eventually, little knobs form that become arms and legs. Up to that point, there is no indication of extremities.

At this time most physical therapists working with cerebral palsy clients or clients who had suffered a stroke, worked only on the extremities (arms and legs). Ed realized that the failures associated with cerebral palsy and strokes could not be fixed by working only on the extremities. The failure meant that somehow things that were learned before birth had been erased. The essence of Ed's theory became that the nervous system must be taken back to the precise point in time and development to correct a background failure. The nervous system must now be taken back to that point in time and development to correct the background failures. The essence of Ed's theory is that these failures cannot be fixed by teaching a physical skill. From that time on Ed worked on background, background and more background. He knew then that failures could not be fixed by teaching a physical skill to a person with background failures.

Ed had discarded about half of the methods he had been taught in physical therapy school because they didn't work. He continued to study and observe babies, children, and adults who gave him insight into some amazing solutions to problems that physical therapists have faced for decades. Through his insight and continued work with a variety of individuals with various problems, Ed gradually developed solutions that provided him with methods to help eliminate learning disabilities in children in public and private schools.

Up until the time of his death in August of 2006, Ed Snapp was always in a discovery mode, making life better for children and adults.

MEMORIES OF ED SNAPP
By Fill Hendrix

Mr. E. A. "Pop" Snapp, Sr., Ed Snapp's father, taught me my first advanced First Aid course while I was teaching elementary physical education in the Clear Creek Schools between Houston and Galveston, Texas. This was in the early sixties. Mr. Snapp was a tremendous teacher, working mostly in the field of physical education at the Y.M.C.A. in Houston and later with the Spring Branch Independent School District. He was truly a "physical educator". He observed with understanding—taking students from where they were, gradually eliminating bad habits and continually encouraging them to realize they could do it all.

During these years, I would see Mr. Snapp from time to time and he would always tell me "You need to meet my son, Ed. He is doing some new and wonderful things in the field of physical therapy." Finally, Ed and I met in my office at the Texas Education Agency in Austin. At that time I was Elementary Physical Education Consultant for Texas.

Ed was involved in working with children with Cerebral Palsy, Down's Syndrome, and other learning disabilities. He told me that he had discarded about half of the methods he had been taught in physical therapy school because they didn't work. As our friendship grew and through Ed's observation, he told me that I probably had problems in following directions and probably had trouble with math in school. I thought, "Who is this guy, anyway!" It was the start of a friendship that lasted nearly 40 years.

Ed and I were determined to get some or all of his methods for eliminating learning disabilities into the curriculum of the public schools of Texas. Little did we know of the obstacles ahead!

The first person I contacted about Ed in north Texas was Marcella Porter, a coordinator of physical education in a school district near

Dallas. She was a personal friend and a member of our state health and physical education association (Texas Association for Health, Physical Education, Recreation and Dance). With the determination of Marcella and Pam Grimes, a teacher in the Dallas area, we began the task of helping Ed set up classes for teachers in Texas. Pam Grimes first used the Snapp methods with her high school varsity tennis team, then with her middle school girls' basketball and track teams, and then with a high school boys' track team. She was convinced that these track teams were able to win several of their track meets because of their increased abilities as a result of these methods. Some principals and other teachers in the schools observed improvements in her students' physical and academic achievements.

Dr. Claudine Sherrill, a professor at Texas Woman's University in Denton, provided the opportunity to hold Ed's first two-week long class in 1975. Across the years, additional classes for teachers and physical therapists were held in various locations in Irving, Austin, Pflugerville, and Houston. Notable among them was the 1977 class in San Marcos at Southwest Texas State University (now Texas State University), where through the efforts of Dr. Jean Smith and Dr. Darlene Schmidt the opportunity was provided for teachers to receive university graduate credit.

We attempted to secure grant funding. Grant money for anything this new and different became impossible. Too many people making the decisions on grants already knew how to do everything "the proper way". Funds, of course, were needed to set up a total program.

In the years to follow, enthusiasm was high among Ed's "graduates", and they moved on to implement as much of the program as possible with their classes as well as with their own children. Chronologically Controlled Developmental Education (CCDE) was born. His graduates used his techniques and methods of presenting materials in various classes (kindergarten, elementary, physical education and special education).

Because of the results of using CCDE techniques professionally, on themselves, and on their family members, the support of his graduates remains high and their enthusiasm continues.

xxx

INTRODUCTION

The purpose of this book is to help **you** build your child into a better learner.

Failure in schoolwork and/or lack of coordinated movements is very frustrating for both you and your child. What can you do? What will work?

We have successfully helped children become more efficient with movement, math, reading, and spelling by using the Snapp approach. This book explains how **you** can also use this program in your home with your child. It explains how to arrange and control the environment to help your child learn.

Ed Snapp called his program "Chronologically Controlled Developmental Education" (CCDE). The basic principle of this program is to begin from the most gross of human activity and progress to very abstract thinking processes.

Ed Snapp said, "Learning begins at conception and continues throughout life." [I-1]

All people have some sort of learning gap. Snapp sought to replace these gaps with learning ability by taking the child through basic human movements. This book will guide you through his methods.

Ed Snapp, Jr., developed CCDE based on the orderly sequence of development (chronological development) of the nervous system within its matching environments.

According to Snapp, genetics provides the structure to function and the environment will determine if the function is successful. Snapp considered the functions of crying, suckling, breathing, crawling, creeping, standing, and walking, as being among our genetic memories that are necessary in order to succeed in one's environment.

As you apply developmental techniques the nervous system will be able to reinforce and/or reestablish genetic memories to make one more successful in his environment. [1-2]

Genetic Memory

Genetic Memory can best be explained by providing an illustration. If you know anything about birds, you can always tell what kind of bird built a given nest. A sparrow never builds an eagle's nest, nor does an oriole ever build a swallow's nest—nor is the young bird given information on constructing the nest. The ability to build the correct nest at the proper time is locked in the bird's genetic memory. So it is with human functions.

Snapp often referred to us as being a magnificent computer system. If properly programmed, this computer is error free—perfect—automatic. Every cell learns a specific function as directed by the genetic code. The developmental clock is turned on at conception, and follows the individual's genetic code until death.

In the womb the sequence of development is fixed by the Genetic Code—unaltered except by chemicals, drugs, serious trauma, illness of the mother, etc. Likewise, after birth a sequence of development by the Genetic Code is fixed. If a child's development is not interrupted by excessive visual or noise stimulation, by limitations of movement, or abnormal contact and interaction with other humans, correct development should continue.

Every human tissue and every human function has a time of initiation, a period of development, and a period of functioning after being "turned on," then a period of decline and, finally, the end of the function or the tissue, or death. Take baby teeth as an example. They appear, serve their purpose, and are lost to make way for the permanent teeth.

Chronological development is precise for all tissues and all functions. During the nine months of uninterrupted fetal development, the sequence of initiation, duration, and cessation of tissues, functions, and sensations are almost identical in all individuals all over the world. Embryologists can determine almost to the day, how old a fetus is according to its stage of development. There is a certain time and a certain sequence when a certain development occurs. If anything is skipped or lost due to trauma, drugs, chemicals, or other means, a function may be lost forever—**unless we can return as closely as possible to the environment and sequence of development in which that function originally began to be developed. Returning to the appropriate environment and activity of a missing function is what CCDE is all about.**

Think of the nervous system as being similar to an electrical circuit. When a fuse blows, or when the breaker switch turns off, the lights will not work. No matter what you do, the lights will not work until the fuse is replaced or the switch is turned back on. In human development, it appears that circuits can be repaired or, if one is damaged permanently, an alternate circuit can be developed—and the sooner, the better.

The theory behind this chronology of development is this: If we can return the nervous system to the time period when a specific developmental process first took place, apparently the nervous system has the ability to scan its own circuits, so to speak, pick out the errors and repair itself. In other words, **the nervous system can detect and correct the problem according to the proper genetic design by replicating the necessary sequence of development within the matching environment.** [I-3]

The goal of the CCDE program, in terms of academic learning, is to present educational material in a way that matches the child's stage of perceptual development to his developmental "age" in an appropriate environment within his neurological tolerance.

If a baby were to develop perfectly and completely he would be a very intelligent and well-coordinated individual. This could mean

3

that his developmental sequence was not interrupted or erased for any reason—like a high fever or drugs. But each one of us has many learning gaps. A method of closing these gaps is to take the body through the basic developmental human movements in chronological order in the proper environment. Going through these movements will re-stimulate the primitive systems (our background) and restore or repair the patterns of movement and sensory reception pathways into the primitive nervous system. When the more primitive systems are in order—that is—when the background is complete, proper sensory input in the appropriate environment will initiate or re-instate function.

Milestones for Motor Skills

Most of us have gaps in the building blocks of our sensory-motor system, our background or "foundation". The development of this background begins at conception, continues throughout the prenatal time period, and forms the groundwork for advanced development known as motor milestones. Roxanne Small, a physical therapist who studied with Ed Snapp, summarizes milestones for certain motor skills listed on developmental charts for infants in her book *Building Babies Better*. [1-4] She points out that the **sequential progression** of these skills is more important than the age at which the child reaches these milestones.

Small's sequential list is as follows:

1. Baby tolerates being on stomach and begins lifting head off the surface.

2. Baby moves arms and legs while on stomach and maintains contact of arms and legs with surface.

3. Baby begins rolling from stomach to back and back to stomach.

4. Baby begins to move on the floor while on belly.

5. Baby pushes onto extended arms while on stomach.

6. Baby gets into a sitting position independently.

7. Baby gets onto hands and knees and begins to rock.

8. Baby begins to creep on hands and knees.

9. Baby begins pulling to stand.

10. Baby begins to cruise walk sideways, holding onto furniture.

11. Baby begins taking independent steps. [I-4]

Sensory-Motor Development

As a parent interested in knowing the impact of activities on your child's development, it is critical that you understand the concept of "sensory-motor" experiences. Our sensory or perceptual systems make us aware of sensations such as sound, taste, visual image, and touch as they pass through our nervous system. Some of the many sensations that we are not usually consciously aware of are; joint position, skin friction, pressure on muscles, tendon stretch, and position in space. How we respond with our muscles to the input from sensations is the motor aspect of sensory-motor development.

It all begins at conception when the single cell receives genetically transferred information that tells it how and when to divide. After that first cell division genetics tells the cells, according to their position, what to learn. In the womb, the feelings of the curled fetal position, warmth, darkness, wetness, slickness, and the sound of mom's heartbeat and blood circulation are basic sensory-motor experiences. After birth seeing natural white light or artificial illumination, feeling dry skin, hearing airborne noise, and stretching out for the first time are more complex abilities, all **built upon** the baby's learning experiences while in the womb or during the birth process.

Most importantly, there is a specific Genetic Code sequence for each of the sensory-motor experiences to be sequentially learned. These experiences create the foundation (building blocks) needed in order for learning to be successful. When more of the early essential sensory-motor experiences are filled in, the foundation is more solid. Building the foundation is a gradual process; but once it is complete, learning is instantaneous.

Five Keys for Sensory-Motor Development [1-5]

Small recommends five keys for good sensory-motor development in an infant:

Key #1: Gross motor comes before fine motor.
Big muscles are developed first to provide a good foundation for smaller muscles to function correctly.

Key #2: Reinforce previous sensory-motor experiences.
Repetition of previously learned sensory-motor experiences is beneficial to help a child organize higher-level skills.

Key #3: Allow baby to grow into higher skills.
Difficulty with a particular skill often indicates a possible problem in a prior foundational sequence.

Key #4: Encourage activities that use both sides of the body.
Provide large toys that require use of both hands to develop the body equally on each side, thus building a good foundation.

Key #5: Avoid small, detailed visual images.
Encourage vision at a distance and avoid over-stimulating the visual system with sustained attention on small details, especially at near distance. [1-5]

Chronologically Controlled Developmental Education (CCDE)

Chronologically Controlled Developmental Education (CCDE) is a teaching/learning method that matches teaching/learning techniques to maturation levels, readiness, and abilities. Snapp summarizes his CCDE processes as follows:

> **Learning is assured when everything that is presented to the child is controlled to be:**
>
> 1) **within the limits of an adequate understanding of background information,**
> 2) **within the limits of perception so that it can be seen, heard, sensed, and understood, and**
> 3) **within the limits before neurological fatigue so that the senses are alert.** (I-6)

Education uses the axiom that large motor activities come first. Yet our current schools concentrate on teaching the child fine motor tasks in the early years. These tasks include coloring within the lines, reading small print, small sized writing, and cutting tasks—all within arms length. (I-7)

CCDE, on the other hand, initially stresses involving the child in large motor skills and initially working at as great a viewing distant as possible when a task involves both visual perception and using one's hands. **If the task involves only visual input, the viewing distance is greater than the length of one's straightened arm.** Education in preschool and up to the third grade should include a majority of large motor elements and longer viewing or working distances for the greatest success in learning. These techniques are appropriate to the physical and social development of the child. (I-8)

Children of all ages will benefit from the activities presented in this book. This CCDE program is set apart from other programs in that it utilizes "before birth sensory-motor concepts and activities" because the concepts identify and the correct activities close gaps

7

in the sensory-motor chronological development. This program provides purposeful, effective, and efficient teaching and learning activities.

The purpose of the CCDE program is to simulate as much as possible an earlier time period to enable the nervous system to re-program its circuits. Most children have gaps in their patterns of sensory-motor development. These gaps can be spotted while watching children as they walk, run, etc., but it takes some practice on the part of the observer to recognize the missing parts of development. Even if one cannot identify the missing function, using CCDE sensory-motor activities in a controlled environment as presented in this book can fill in gaps and reinforce correct development.

Snapp based his work on the belief that replication of genetic developmental movements and sensations in a matching controlled environment allows the nervous system to return to an earlier time period. According to Snapp's theory, when the nervous system is provided with the environment and sensations of an earlier time period it can scan its own circuits, find the problems, and reprograms itself. [1-9] Strange as it may seem, this apparently happens.

References

I-1. Snapp, Edward A., Jr., P. T., Workshop materials beginning in 1975.

I-2. Snapp, Edward A., Jr., P.T., The Language of Life, Health, Rehabilitation, Unpublished paper, 1990; made available by Ed's daughter, Susan Snapp.

I-3. Schmidt, Darlene, Parent Handbook, unpublished paper presented to parents of students involved in CCDE program at Southwest Texas State University, San Marcos, Texas, 1983.

I-4. Small, Roxanne, P.T., *Building Babies Better, Developing a Solid Foundation for Your Child*, Trafford Pub., Victoria, BC, Canada, 2005, pp. 5-6.

I-5. ibid, p. 15.

I-6. Snapp, Edward A., Jr., P.T., Chronologically Controlled Developmental Education, Unpublished paper, 1983, p. 18; made available by Ed's daughter, Susan Snapp.

I-7. Ward, Betty J., Maximum Available Desk-to-Eye Distance for Students in Grades One and Two, Unpublished doctoral dissertation, 1989, Texas Woman's University, Denton, Texas; Internet: Betty J. Ward, PhD.

I-8. Alff, Lucy, Developmental Education, unpublished paper prepared for classroom teachers, 1977, p. 1.

I-9. Snapp, Edward A., Jr., P. T., course materials beginning in July, 1975.

SNAPP CCDE PRINCIPLES

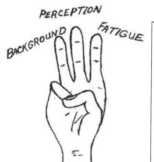

BACKGROUND: Stay within the child's developmental and educational background.

PERCEPTION: Stay within child's perceptual level for each of his senses.

FATIGUE: Stop before fatigue of the nervous system is apparent.

Introduction

Do you know of a good athlete who cannot function in the classroom? It is as if he has "not hatched yet". As Ed Snapp observed these types of individuals, as well as the spastic movements of some children, he thought, possibly, that given the right opportunity the nervous system would correct itself—"fix it".

Snapp theorized these individuals needed to go back to an earlier time period so that the nervous system would remember and complete development from an earlier time period, and work from there. Gradually Snapp was able to distinguish one prenatal movement from another prenatal movement. He placed these distinguishable movements on a time line. This time line enabled him to (1) better visualize a chronology of development encompassing specific movements, function, and/or environment and (2) to realize that these specifics were required and necessary to allow the nervous system to "think" it was back in an earlier developmental time of the human genetic code.

Snapp used this time line in his classes to emphasize that there is a proper developmental sequence of activities, with little variation from one individual to another, from conception to death. Snapp continuously emphasized that for each of the developmental activities there is a required matching environment that is essential for development to take place.

The following are the SNAPP CCDE Principles and their definitions that will be used in this book.

SNAPP CCDE Principles
(Chronologically Controlled Developmental Education)

Awareness
Physical maturation precedes awareness. Awareness (perceiving the absence or presence of a given sensory input) precedes the initiation of a function. Function precedes understanding. Therefore, awareness is required for learning and development to occur.

Developmental Environment
A setting that is concerned with the temperature, light, sound, tactile sensations, and other sensory conditions associated with the specific developmental activity. This environment affects both physical maturation and function. The matching controlled environment is necessary to reprogram the nervous system for developmental learning.

There is a proper developmental and/or a redevelopment of a sequence of activities and for each of the activities there is a required matching environment essential for development to take place.

Background
A completed background of development is the cornerstone for all human functions. The CCDE presentation methods build upon the fully developed prenatal, natal and neonatal background of the child's understanding.

A function is both correct and efficient or there are gaps in the background of development. **If an observed function is incorrect in any degree, a return to an earlier developmental pattern leads to the solution.**

Perception
Inaccurate perception in hearing, seeing, and other sensory input can result in unintended responses. Accurate perceptions are not inborn qualities but must be learned or developed.

Fatigue
The nervous system has a fatigue factor. Neurological fatigue causes the intended learning to stop or results in errors in the understanding and in the correct response. It is nervous system fatigue that is of greatest concern, and it is the first fatigue to occur. This text uses "fatigue" and "neurological fatigue" interchangeably and in each instance refers to neurological fatigue.

Chronology
Chronological order of academic learning of any subject is as follows:
  recognition,
  echo of information,
  fill in the blank,
  single facts,
  multiple facts,
  comparison,
  analysis,
  projection.

Successful Results
The key to successful learning is having the instructional presentation: within the child's background, within the child's level of perception, and before the child becomes too fatigued for the nervous system to understand and respond correctly.

SNAPP's Dimensions

Ed Snapp used the term "Dimension" in describing levels of abilities. He used this term because dimension is related to the physical relation of the child to his environment. That is, when the child is static in space, not yet having the ability to move across space, the child's relationship to space is or has only One Dimension (1D). When he begins to move across space on his stomach, the child has the Two Dimension (2D) relationship to his use of or movement through space. When he gets up on all fours (Creeping), he now has the Three Dimension (3D) relationship to his use of or movement in space: he is raised from the surface as well as moving across or through space. The Four Dimension and Five Dimension begin to employ use of the child's thoughts, which can move him through different levels of thinking, first going from simple concepts through analysis, and then to projection of thoughts asking "What if" and then to projecting possible outcomes. *Building Better Learners* does not go beyond Three Dimension. For additional information about SNAPP's Dimensions, see Appendix A.

The four subject areas in this book are: 1) Foundation of Movement, 2) Visual Perception, 3) Chronology of Reading, Writing, and Spelling, and 4) Chronology of Math. The subject areas in this book incorporate the use of Snapp's 1D, 2D, and 3D levels. The 1D activities presented are the BACKGROUND for all other Dimensions. The 1D activities are the beginning activities of each subject area and should be completed with at least 90% accuracy before 2D activities are begun. The same criteria apply to 2D activities before starting 3D activities.

All 1D activities in a subject area need to be completed before moving to the 2D activities in that subject area. For example, all 1D activities in the Foundation of Movement Chapter need to be completed before moving to the 2D activities in the Foundation of Movement Chapter. The same criteria apply to 2D activities before starting 3D activities. It is important to remember that these criteria apply to any academic area as well as to any physical activity.

It was Snapp's intent to complete all 1D activities in all subject areas before moving on to 2D activity in any subject area. We understand that your situation is unique and may be suited to moving your child through 1D, 2D, or even 3D activities in one subject area while working with him until he reaches 90% accuracy in another subject at the 1D level. So, depending on your situation, your child could be working at a 2D or 3D level in one subject area while developing background at the 1D level in another subject area.

Thus, Snapp's method of CCDE guarantees learning.

The Three-Finger Salute

BACKGROUND, PERCEPTION, FATIGUE

Always keep these three essential
principles in mind.

(1-1)

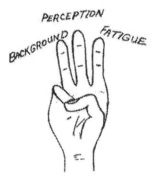

Background
A fully developed background for each activity is critical to progress. An incorrect outcome is a red flag to start at a level lower than the material being presented. For example, if handwriting, catching, or reading are not done well, do not continue working on them. Instead, go back in developmental time to basic light stimulation, eye-hand

tracking, pre-crawling, and/or earlier **SNAPP** Cards to build the background for forward progress.

Presentation of the material demonstrated should be at the child's level of understanding. This is verified by his ability to incorporate the accurate performance of the activity **automatically** in the next developmental level. He does not have to "think about it" in order to be successful. Exceeding the child's level of understanding will leave gaps in education and/or coordination. Background development is the cornerstone of all more complex developments. Leave no gaps!

One of Snapp's examples of the significance of background is his auto assembly line story:

> If a car rolls off the assembly line and it is missing door handles because it was accelerated past Station 9 where door handle installation occurs, the outcome is that the car will always lack door handles.

> In an effort to complete the car's assembly the car is rolled back down the assembly line to Station 10 and **the following work is done:**
> Station 10: Tighten the windshield wipers, check air in the tires and test the horn.
> **Result:** car is still missing door handles.
> **Solution:** Roll the car back down the assembly line to Station 9 where door handles are installed.
> **Result:** car has door handles, windshield wipers are retightened, the air in tires is rechecked and the horn is retested.
> **Terminal result:** car has door handles and everything that comes after installation of door handles has been reinforced. The car's background is complete.

> Now, what was the result when the car was rolled back down the assembly line beyond Station 10 to Station 9 (time and environment for door handle installation)? **Result:** Door handles were installed (at Station 9) and every function that had already been done at Station 10 (retighten the windshield wipers,

recheck air in tires, and retest the horn) was reinforced. The car's background is complete, and with no gaps. [1-2]

There is no advantage to acceleration until the background is complete. [1-3]

Perception
Perception is the ability to understand basic sensory input. Perception is how the child receives, processes, and reacts to his sensory input. Learning takes place in connection with the ability to perceive information correctly. Lack of correct awareness of the sound of voice, visual input, sensing pressure on or within the body, or positional input will result in learning errors and incorrect responses. These types of learning errors indicate a need to go back in developmental time to the **most basic sensory input.**

Fatigue
"Fatigue", as used by Ed Snapp, refers to neurological fatigue, not muscular fatigue. Neurological fatigue interferes with the processing of information and often occurs when a child has worked too long at a given task at the present stage of his development. The nervous system has an endurance factor so that neurological fatigue causes mistakes to be made. When mistakes begin to be made after a period of success, stop that activity! Change to a different task, a different environment, or use the body in a different way.

When the child is learning successfully, you are working within his developmental background and perception level. When neurological fatigue occurs, errors will follow. Fatigue may occur within a few seconds for some children. Neurological fatigue will be less frequent as the child's background abilities continue to develop.

Note the length of activity time when neurological fatigue sets in, for it will vary from individual to individual. **DO NOT** continue into fatigue. Continuing the same learning activity when a child is fatigued makes learning more difficult because errors will be made; the error then becomes what is learned. To continue is non-productive.

The perfect learning situation is when the child's background is complete, the sequence of materials presented is correct and the child perceives all material correctly. When we reach the point of fatigue the nervous system deviates and the child begins to make errors. [I-4]

> Practice does not make perfect; practice is repetition of what one knows or of what one does not know. [1-5]

Practice after learning occurs is beneficial to strengthening that nervous system connection to allow that connection to retrieve the correct response faster.

Learning is instantaneous when both the material presented and the presentation methods are within the child's perception, background, and without fatigue. Gaps in learning and immature behavior occur if one or more of the following are present:

1) the child's background is exceeded,
2) presentation is outside of the child's level of perception, or
3) the child is too fatigued for the nervous system to understand.

References

1-1. Snapp, Edward A., Jr., P.T., Graduate Course/Workshop, Southwest Texas State University, San Marcos, Texas, July, 1977.

1-2. Snapp, Edward A., Jr., P.T., Texas Woman's University Graduate Course, Denton, Texas, July, 1975.

1-3. Snapp, Edward A., Jr., P.T., CCDE Course, Pflugerville, Texas, 1979.

1-4. Grimes, Pam, Notes from Ed Snapp on fatigue as reflected from class shorthand notes taken by Pam Grimes at a CCDE Course, Pflugerville, Texas, 1979.

1-5. Snapp, Edward A., Jr., P.T., unpublished paper presented at Texas Woman's University Graduate Course, Denton, Texas, June, 1975.

FOUNDATION OF MOVEMENT

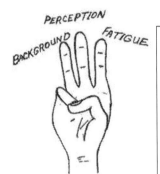

BACKGROUND: Stay within the child's developmental and educational background.

PERCEPTION: Stay within child's perceptual level for each of his senses.

FATIGUE: Stop before fatigue of the nervous system is apparent.

<u>SNAPP Principle</u>: **A completed background of development is the cornerstone for all human functions. The CCDE presentation methods build upon the developed background of the child's understanding and continue to make it stronger.**

Human Learning

There are patterns to human learning. These patterns or processes are genetically bound since we all know how to do them. We were not taught instinctive patterns of crying, suckling, breathing, crawling, creeping, standing, walking, etc. These are genetic memories locked in our development.

We learn our first movements prenatally, even before we look human. As we learn each of these movements the correlating cells of the nervous system puts these movements together so that they can be used automatically either separately or in any combination.

Learning begins at conception. The learning process is a continuing process. In our genetic code there is a certain time to learn each specific function. This learning provides the background for the next sequential development.

Snapp's knowledge of human physiology allowed him to envision prenatal development. He initially reasoned and later determined that prenatal activities serve as developmental background for future learning that occurs at birth and thereafter.

Starting from simple movements and progressing to more complex movements is a developmental process. Once a developmental process is learned it then becomes the background for the next learning process.

At birth the baby encounters new and different environments and different learning situations. At birth the baby has more space in which to move. The patterns in his genetic code contain all prenatal and postnatal movements that lead to crawling on the stomach, which leads to sitting, creeping on hands and knees, standing, walking, and other sensory-motor activities. It is from these genetically bound activities that one progresses into playing games, sports, and—most importantly, lifetime movement.

It is established that humans follow a genetic code of development. Sensations are integrated and movement is sequentially developed during prenatal and natal (birth process) times as one progresses under the direction of the genetic code. So it appears possible to use developmental controls and developmental activities to affect gaps in one's genetic code of development.

Although many developmental activities in this book may seem too simple, it is essential that they be included to build the necessary background for successful academics and lifetime movements. Starting at the most basic level assures that one's background and perceptions are complete. This sequential method builds the nervous system's endurance to reduce fatigue for academic and physical activities.

If at any time the child cannot grasp the concepts, information, or activities presented, gaps exist in his development. It is necessary that information and matching environment of an earlier time period be presented to fill in these gaps. As a parent using the CCDE methods with her son commented, "There are no short cuts. Take time to go through each step, working at the child's pace." Margie Boyd [2-1]

Make sure that the child's understanding is complete. "Complete understanding" is demonstrated by his being able to incorporate the accurate performance of one developmental level of activity **automatically** into the next developmental level. That is; he does not "have to think about it" in order to employ it to be successful.

In working with these movements there is limited or no talking by the child or the adult. The sensations received by the child's body and perceived by him are the basis for progress for learning. Talking interferes with the perception and integration of the sensations. **Therefore, verbal directions are kept at a minimum.**

Giving verbal directions takes the child's attention off what his body is sensing and makes the child manage his body by consciously thinking. "Thinking about it" is not part of the internal developmental environment. The nervous system must perceive the sensations and movements on a lower ability than thinking and/or seeing in order to build awareness, assimilate it, and use it automatically. However, if verbal directions are necessary, give the directions before the child starts to move. Thereafter, the adult positions the body part without comment.

About the Environment

The learning environment in which a child is working is relevant to the developmental progress. The environment should be correlated with the developmental activity. The room might be quiet and dimly lit with the source of the light not shining directly on the child while working on developmental movements on and across a surface. The child should not be aware of the source of the light. **Since all fluorescent lights have a flicker and some of these lights have a sound, they should be avoided.**

The **developmental environment** is a unique setting that is concerned with the temperature, light, sound, surface, and other sensory conditions associated with the specific developmental activity.

Visual, auditory, and tactile distractions (pictures on the wall, television or radio, cell phone, computer or I-pod, toys or pets) should not be allowed in the room with the child. Even odors, snacks, and/or drinks, or the clothes the child or the adult is wearing, can be distracting. Blinds or curtains should cover the windows so outside activity or outside lighting does not become a distraction. Room temperature should be comfortable. Having no internal or external environmental distractions allows more focus on learning perception of both the external and internal sensory inputs.

A firm, slick, and smooth surface without texture is best for basic patterns when the child is on his stomach for an activity. This makes for a great **crawling surface** in that it allows movement across the surface with as little resistance as possible. Ceramic tiled floors are not suitable surfaces for crawling because they have breaks between individual tiles whereas a child should be sensing a smooth rigid surface with the palm of his hand. Also, tiles are sometimes uneven. Carpet is never a suitable surface for crawling because carpet has texture. The child senses this texture as a rough surface and a rough surface is never the right environment for crawling. The best crawling surface is smooth, slick, rigid, and without a distracting design. A wooden floor is a great **crawling surface.**

If only a carpeted, embossed or grouted tile surface is available, a smooth, slick vinyl crawling surface can easily be made. A 6' x 9' sheet of vinyl, purchased from a carpet store, can be cut in half lengthwise creating two pieces 3' x 9'. Use packaging tape on the underside to hold the two surfaces together, creating an area of 3' x 18'. Place this vinyl over the floor area for the basic patterns and for crawling activities that follow. Another way to make the slick, smooth surface is to use FRP (fiberglass reinforced panel) board, which comes in 4' x 8' panels.

Comfortable smooth clothing without buttons, zippers, ties, belts, or jewelry is necessary while performing developmental activities. Sweatpants and top would be the appropriate attire for some activities. Be sure there is no jewelry worn or that there is nothing on the clothing that will interfere with developmental activities or movement across a surface. Other activities require bare skin of given body parts.

When the child is on his back performing flexion activities he should be lying on a mat to protect the spine.

Sensations and Movement Patterns

The sensations and movement patterns that follow are integrated into more complex movement patterns as the child progresses through his development. If possible, activity sessions should be performed three to five days per week. These sessions reinforce learning and understanding of developmental movements.

The sequence of movement activities presented in this book is a compilation from Ed Snapp's teachings, beginning in the 1970's. This information can also be found in his unpublished paper "Developmental Learning", 2002. [2.2] **Snapp emphasized that there is a proper developmental sequence of activities. For each of the developmental activities there is a required matching environment that is essential for development to take place.**

In this Chapter, Foundation of Movement, the activities start with the most basic 1D (One Dimension) activities before progressing to more complex activities of 2D (Two Dimension) and 3D (Three Dimension). Each 1D activity should be completed at a minimum of 90% accuracy before moving into any 2D activities. The same criteria apply to moving from 2D activities into 3D activities. Completion of 1D activities at the minimum of 90% accuracy provides a good foundation to building a better learner. Completion of any activity at a greater percentage of accuracy provides an even greater foundation for your child to build upon to reach his potential.

For more information on **SNAPP**'s Dimensions refer to page 14, or to Dimensions listed in the Glossary, or Appendix A.

A. Flexion Positioning (1D)

Concept to be Learned: Flexion, Adduction, and Inward Rotation (Text Box 201)

1. Goal of exercise: • have nervous system learn and/or reinforce flexion, adduction and inward rotation • build trunk stability 2. What is needed: • bean bag chair or mat with pillows to support neck and head • recommended: heart beat/ blood flow recording without music	3. The environment: • quiet, dark area 4. Position of the child: • on back in tight tuck position 5. Number of repetitions: (length of time) • position maintained for up to 45 minutes (good place/time for a nap) 6. How many times day/week: • 3 times a week • more is better; benefit never ends

While resting quietly in the fetal position (flexed, adducted, and inwardly rotated) in a dark, comfortable, warm environment, it is possible for the nervous system to remember an earlier time and environment. During the first nine months (prenatal life) flexion, adduction, and inward rotation were developed; prenatal time is the only time when these movement patterns are initiated and developed. The fetal position and the quiet, dark environment allows the nervous system to go back to this specific time and environment to learn, relearn, and/or reinforce what positions and movements it did during prenatal development.

To place the child in the fetal position, a beanbag chair can be used to position the child on his back, knees bent with his feet resting on the wall or the inside "wall" of the beanbag. A pillow is placed under the head and shoulders to enhance the flexion.

When a beanbag chair is not available, the child may lie on his back on a mat, with several pillows under his head and feet so as to place him in a position with his neck, trunk, hips and knees flexed. The environment is dark.

Flexed Position in Beanbag Chair

Optimally, a recording of a heart beat and blood movement, without music is played while he is in this position in the dark environment. In the child's environment before birth there was auditory input to the child both from within and without the mother's body. The recording played during the session in the beanbag is used to replicate the prenatal sounds heard by the fetus while within the mother. These recordings, without music, can be found in maternity or baby shops. If possible, keep the child in this environment for up to 45 minutes. The beanbag chair is an excellent place to take a nap. **Do not leave child unattended.**

Initially Snapp used a large car inner tube to create the fetal position within the uterine environment. He cleaned and split the entire inner circle of the tube so that the child could sit in a flexed position inside the tube. The surface and shape of the tube simulated the confined environment of the womb. He suspended the tube so that it hung a few inches from the floor when the child was inside. The emphasis in this environment was the fetal position.

However, while in this position inside the tube the child will move some in order to be more comfortable. As he extends his hips, knees, and ankles, he pushes against the inner surface of the tube. In doing so, flexion of the neck and trunk increases. Snapp would caution the child to relax slowly, so that the knees would not rebound quickly, for a sudden relaxation could cause the knees to hit his face. As the child extends the neck and trunk and pushes backward against the tube, the flexion of the hips, knees and ankles increases. Some children are very active while in the tube and repeat the action over and over while other children go to sleep while in this environment.

DO NOT LEAVE THE CHILD UNATTENDED AT ANY TIME!

B. Surface Sensations

1. Light Touch (1D)
Concept to be Learned: Light Touch (Text Box 202)

1. Goal of exercise:
  • allow the release of flexion adduction and inward rotation
  • help one to both perceive and understand surfaces
  • perceive sensations that are necessary for learning
2. What is needed:
  • mat or smooth padded surface
  • wet, oiled, or bare skin
	3. The environment:
	  • quiet, dimly lit area
	4. Position of the child:
	  • on back, eyes closed
	  • arms on chest, palms open
	  • knees raised and bent, legs together
	5. Number of repetitions:
	  • 10 to 20
	6. How many times day/week:
	  • 3 times per week
	  • more is better; benefit never ends

Light Touch:
> allows the release of flexion, adduction, and inward rotation, helps one to both perceive and understand surfaces, and enables extension, abduction, and outward rotation.

27

Light touch is first experienced while the child is in the womb as he moves through the amniotic fluid. After birth light touch is integrated best when it is skin on skin. Skin sensation is more intense at bath time because moistening the skin with water, oil, or lotion creates slick surfaces. When not in a bath, light touch can be done by having the child in a loose-fitting shirt, barefooted, and wearing shorts while doing the arm movements under the shirt—skin to skin. If modesty is not an issue when working in a home setting, the child can be with bare chest as he does the light touch movements.

a. Light Touch Leg Rubs
The adult first moves the child through the following reciprocating leg movement then verbally cues him at the appropriate time to, "Relax." The child relaxes, with feet flat on the floor, knees bent, and open hands on his chest. After a short relaxation period, the adult raises the child's feet and legs to the starting position, and cues the child by saying, "Now you do it."

In a dimly lit room the child is on a mat or similar surface to protect the spine. The child lies on his back with eyes closed. His elbows are flexed and arms are on his chest with palms and fingers open, and knees raised and bent. The child holds his legs so that the front of the lower legs is parallel to the ceiling with his feet in the air. He holds the feet, ankles, and knees lightly together, his legs are not crossed, and the inner surfaces of the legs are in light contact with one another. He lightly rubs his lower legs, knees, and feet together in back and forth movements with short slow strokes for about 30 seconds (between 10-20 times). Do not count out loud nor permit the child to count. Relax and rest bottom of feet on the floor with knees and hips flexed.

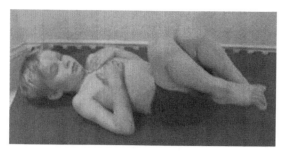

Leg Rubs

The focus of leg rubs is the sensory input and perception of the light touch. Speed is not the intended purpose.

Leg Rubs enhance and coordinate the alternating movement of the legs as in crawling, walking, running, skipping, bicycling, some swimming patterns, etc. As the legs rub together the hips, knees, and toes will be orientated in the proper straightforward position. The head can be supported by a pillow or remain on the mat. The adult is observing to ensure that the child's legs and feet are lightly touching as they rub together. If the limbs are not touching lightly, gently move the legs to correct the position without comment to the child.

Some children may have difficulty maintaining the position for leg rubs. If this is the case, leg rubs may be done while the child lies on his side in the fetal position and slides the top leg back and forth on the stationary bottom leg. More sensory input will be received by a child in this resting position than when unsuccessfully struggling to maintain a balanced position on his back or when struggling to keep his legs held up.

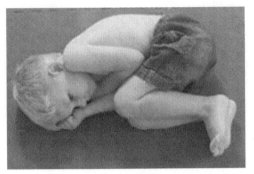

Leg Rub: Side Fetal Position

Change position to the other side and have the child do leg rubs on that side as well.

b. Light Touch Arm Rubs with Hand Moving to Outside of Hip
In a quiet dimly lit room the child should be on a mat or similar surface to protect the spine. The child lies on his back with eyes closed. His arms are on his chest with palms and fingers relaxed and open, hips and knees bent, with feet flat on the floor.

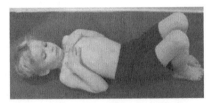

Starting Position

 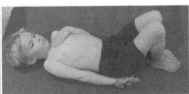

Across the Chest   In Contact with Hip
Light Touch Arm Rub Sequence

The adult moves the child through the following movement, and then tells the child, "Now you do it."

The left hand and arm remain stationary against the left side of the chest. The child's right hand starts to move across the chest, extends at the elbow to slide to the side as it inwardly rotates, and slides down the trunk, to the outside of the hip. The **entire length of the arm** stays in contact with the body as the arm extends and slowly inwardly rotates; the open hand rotates so that the back of the hand (knuckle side) comes in contact with the outside of the hip. As the elbow is straightened the arm rotates at the shoulder. These rotations cause the back of the hand to be against the body when the hand reaches the outer hip. The adult should make sure that the elbow remains in contact with the side of the chest at all times.

As the right hand slides back up across the body and chest it returns to starting position with the palm of the hand and arm again on the chest. Repeat exercise 5 times.

The child repeats exercise 5 times with the left arm.

c. Light Touch Arm Rubs with Hand Moving Inside of Thigh
The child lies on his back in the fully flexed position with his eyes closed and his feet flat on the floor. Or he may lie on his back in the flexed position with his head supported on a pillow, and his feet up against the wall. Refer to starting position on page 30.

The adult moves the child through the following movements, and then tells the child, "Now you do it."

Both arms are flexed and resting on the chest. One arm extends downward and inwardly rotates as the arm pushes downward and inwardly rotates between the thighs. Resistance to arm extension is greater when the arm moves to the inside of the thigh than when the arm moves to the outside of the hip.

When the arm is fully extended and inwardly rotated the arm is then outwardly rotated as it returns upward to the starting position. This Light Touch Inside Thigh movement builds arm muscles. Repeat arm rub with each arm 5 times.

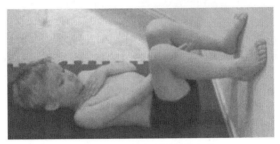

Light Touch Inside Thigh

The elbow extension and the arm and shoulder rotations used in Arm Rubs are the same movements that are used in swimming, overhand throwing, and in serving for tennis or volleyball. Thus, these complex sports activities are enhanced with the use of Light Touch Arm Rubs moving to the outside of the hip and/or extending between the thighs.

Either of the above Arm Rubs may also be done as the child lies on his side in the fetal position. Have the child change position to the other side and do Arm Rubs on that side as well.

2. Pounding (1D) and Rubbing (2D)

In this exercise as well as other exercises in this book, the suggested sitting position of the child is with legs crossed. However, if your child cannot sit cross-legged or needs to change his position, he may sit in a chair or on the floor in a position more comfortable to him.

Concept to be Learned: Use of the Palm (Text Box 203)

1. Goal of exercise:
  • relaxation in the hands
  • developmental founda-
    tion for handwriting
  • enables finger extension
  • create body sensations
    that are necessary for
    learning
2. What is needed:
  • hard flat surface
	3. The environment:
	  • quiet, dimly lit area
	4. Position of the child:
	  • sitting cross-legged on
	    floor or sitting at a table
	  • palms flat
	5. Number of repetitions:
	  • minimum of 10 times
	6. How many times day/week:
	  • 3 times per week
	  • more is better
	  • benefit never ends

The adult demonstrates the activity of pounding with the palm and then introduces the activity of rubbing the palm and forearm across surfaces to the child. Then tells the child, "Now you do it."

a) The child, sitting with legs crossed, leans forward to pound the palm of one hand on the floor or flat surface. The child extends his fingers slightly backward so that only the palm is striking the floor. The child pounds vigorously and forcefully on the surface 10 times. The child then rubs the palm of the hand back and forth on the flat surface. Repeat with the other hand.

b) While sitting at a table with a smooth surface, the child uses one hand to pound his palm on the surface several times. The child then rubs the palm of the hand back and forth on the flat surface. Repeat with the other hand.

c) Then with the inner forearm (elbow to palm) in contact with the surface, the child rubs the forearm in various patterns. The trunk remains stationary with movement coming from the shoulder. Repeat with the other hand and forearm.

Pounding builds the child's awareness of hand and arm sensation. These pounding and rubbing movements using the entire arm from shoulder to palm are the developmental foundation for handwriting and drawing.

Over time and with repeated pounding, this activity will stimulate a sense of relaxation in the hands.

3. Spatial Relations Rub (2D)

Concept to be Learned: Using the palm to understand contoured surfaces (Text Box 204)

1. Goal of exercise: • to perceive and understand surfaces • to understand contoured surfaces through use of palm of hand and finger joints (not FINGER TIPS) • gives sense of body awareness • stimulates and integrates both sides of the brain 2. What is needed: • no specified equipment	3. The environment: • quiet, dimly lit area 4. Position of the child: • sitting, standing, or reclining 5. Number of repetitions: • one complete pattern of the body parts listed 6. How many times day/week: • 3 times a week • more is better • benefit never ends

During these exercises the child's palm and base of his fingers will contour around the body parts being rubbed, with the most important contact to be placed on the palm and curved joints of the fingers. The tips of the fingers are not used.

The adult models the rubbing of her hands together then says to the child "Do this with me." The adult rubs her hands together long enough to make them warm, then claps her hands together three times. The child mirrors the adult as she uses the warm palm and curved fingers of one hand to rub the following body areas in a brisk manner:
forearm (wrist to elbow),
elbow to shoulder,
on the shoulder,
on the thigh (knee to hip),
on other thigh (knee to hip),
on the stomach,
across the entire front of the chest,
one side of neck,
other side of neck,
on one cheek,
on other cheek

Rub hands together again, clap three times and repeat all on opposite side of the body using the other palm and curved fingers. Allow time for the child to participate in the sequence. Eventually, the child will learn the sequence of this contoured surface activity. He can then do this activity anytime on his own.

REMEMBER: Fingertips are not used in this activity.

Another way to better understand contoured surfaces is to use the palm and joints of curved fingers of one hand to briskly rub contoured surfaces found around the house and then repeat this activity with the palm and joints of curved fingers on the other hand. Examples of contoured surfaces around the house are the arms of a sofa, the arms of a chair, cushions, the edge of a bed, columns, curved lamp bases, curved table legs, paper towel rolls, and curved railings.

C. Deep Pressure Stimulation (1D)

Concept to be Learned: Understanding the Sensation of Deep Pressure (Text Box 205)

*If you can do only one physical activity, this is the one!

1. Goal of exercise:
 • improve postural control
 • develop body awareness
 • balance muscle
   sensation and muscle
   function
 • increase muscle tone
 • create body sensations
   that are necessary for
   learning
 • calm hyperactivity
 • reduce lethargy
	2. What is needed:
	 • mat or smooth surface
	3. The environment:
	 • quiet, dimly lit area
	4. Position of the child:
	 • varied, depending on
	   area being stimulated
	5. Number of repetitions:
	 • twice a day if possible
	6. How many times day/week:
	 • daily, more is better
	 • benefit never ends

Much of the following explanation of deep pressure is paraphrased from *Building Babies Better* by permission of the author, Roxanne Small, P. T. [2.3]

Understanding of skin sensations and muscle tissue awareness is critical to the total development of a coordinated child. Deep pressure stimulates deep sensations. It is felt more by the muscles than by the skin. Deep pressure is done by gently pushing your thumb, the tip of a finger, or a device (such as one tip of the massage "star" available in stores) into the child's muscle until the bone is felt.

36

Deep pressure is a balancer of muscle tone. Deep pressure sensation is capable of decreasing tight muscle tone and helping the muscles to relax. Additionally, deep pressure sensation is capable of increasing low muscle tone, reducing loose flabby muscles and developing strong muscles. Deep pressure is done in a quiet dimly lit room with the child in one of three possible positions: lying on his tummy, held in the adult's arms, or held against the adult's chest.

Do not do deep pressure on the biceps (front of the upper arms), abdomen, inner surface of the thighs, or the calves (back of lower legs). The stomach and intestines are not made to handle deep pressure. Deep pressure on the biceps, inner surface of the thighs or on the calves may give a negative result (increase muscle tone where relaxation is needed). Do not do pressure on the joints.

Only enough pressure is applied to go through the muscle to touch the bone gently. Where there is less muscle, less pressure is used. During the first session start out gently and slowly. Progressively, more pressure is added at each session. Do one area at a time. Pressure on the back or arms is usually better tolerated than pressure on the legs.

Some children will not like deep pressure at first but come to tolerate it, and then like it. Before a child's nervous system understands and enjoys deep pressure, he may:

1) have no response
2) perceive being tickled, or
3) be irritated or perceive it as being painful.

Eventually he will tolerate and accept this sensory experience as his nervous system develops and begins to understand it. Deep pressure will build balanced muscle tone and great body awareness.

If a child perceives deep pressure as being painful, this is not a signal to stop. The perception of pain is part of the developmental process. Try doing only one body part at a session and do a different body part at another time. Consistent use of deep pressure will build a child's tolerance for it and will reap many benefits. Deep pressure can help one to fall asleep, calm down, or focus on studies. As deep pressure sensation becomes completely integrated, the pressure will feel good to the individual.

Because deep pressure is so valuable in helping the nervous system develop, it should be done no less than twice a day. There is often a residual sensation from deep pressure that lasts from five to twenty minutes. Therefore it is helpful to do the pressure before doing other developmental activities. Usually all deep pressure points can be completed in five to ten minutes. [2.3]

Snapp states that there are various responses to a child's perception of pressure. He describes these responses as first having no awareness of the pressure, then awareness of and perceiving it as being ticklish or irritating; later followed by being enjoyable.

In his writings Snapp further states that deep pressure stimulation not only improves muscle, tendon, and skin sensations, but the pressure also stimulates the covering of the bones (periostium of the bone). Therefore the pressure applied needs to be deep enough so as to reach the sensory receptors on the bone lining. To be effective, press the thumb through the muscle until the muscle is pressing firmly against the bone.

Pressure stimulation is given while holding the child or as the child rests face down on a mat or carpet in a dimly lighted room. The areas of muscles to be stimulated are:

the palm of each hand,
the top and the bottom of each forearm,

the back of each upper arm,
the muscles which run along each side of the backbone
(pressure on the entire length),
the sole of each foot,
the inside arch of each foot, and
the front, outer side, and back of each thigh. (2.4)

Points for Deep Pressure
Back

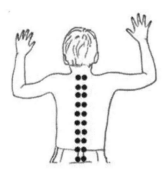

Begin deep pressure on the back by pressing at the base of the neck on one side, starting on the muscles one inch out from the spine. Move about an inch farther down the muscle along the side of the spine, applying pressure after each move until you reach the muscles by the tailbone. Stay on the muscles and not on the bony area of the spine.

Repeat on the other side of the spine. **Do not press on spine.**

Hands and Arms

The hand and arm areas are best done with the child lying face down on a comfortable surface. Do all pressure points on one hand and arm completely, then do all pressure points on the other hand and arm.

Palm

Press into the fleshy part of the palm. Press into the outer edges and into the center of the palm. Think of a pattern of about nine points; do the outer surface of the palm in rectangular fashion, then do the point in the center of the palm.

Inside of Forearm

On the inside of the forearm, begin pressure at the wrist and continue as you move your fingers or thumb up about an inch at a time, all the way to the elbow. Apply pressure after each move.

Back of Upper Arm

Start pressing just above the back of the elbow on the back of the upper arm. Move upward about an inch at a time, applying pressure after each move. Do not apply pressure to the shoulder. Do pressure **only** on the **back** of the upper arm.

Top of Forearm

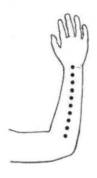

On the top of the forearm, begin pressure at the wrist and continue as you move your fingers or thumb up about an inch at a time, all the way to the elbow. Apply pressure after each move.

Repeat all pressure points on the other hand and arm.

Feet and Legs

Do all pressure points on one foot and leg completely. Then do all pressure points on the other foot and leg.

Foot

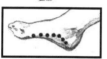

Press into the sole of the foot, moving completely around the edges of the foot. Apply pressure up through the middle of the sole. Press on the inner side of the foot from the joint of the big toe to the heel, following the arch. When moving to a new position on the foot, make the move about an inch from the previous position.

Back Of Upper Leg (Thigh)

Apply pressure to the back of the upper leg, moving from the knee upward to the middle of the buttocks. Start just above one of the dimples on the back of the knee, moving upward into the middle of the buttock. Move upward about an inch at a time, applying pressure after each move. Repeat, starting above the other dimple in the back of the knee.

Reposition the leg so that both the relaxed hip and knee are bent out to the side at approximately 90-degrees. The child is lying face down; the front of the trunk and pelvis, the inner side of the knee, lower leg, and foot are resting on the flat surface. The following picture indicates the position of the pressure points. If the child cannot release flexion enough to have the trunk and pelvis flat on the surface while the hip and leg are in this position, he needs more of light touch experiences.

Outside Of Upper Leg (Thigh)

Apply pressure on the **outside of the upper leg**, moving from just above the knee to the hip joint. Move upward about an inch at a time, applying pressure after each move.

Front Of Upper Leg (Thigh)

With the child lying on his back, arms to the side, apply pressure to the front of the upper leg from just above the knee upward to the front of the hip. Move upward about an inch at a time, applying pressure after each move.

Repeat all pressure points on the other foot and leg.

Eventually a child learns the sequence of Deep Pressure Stimulation and can then apply deep pressure everywhere on himself but on his back.

D. Flexion

1. Quick Tucks (1D)

Concept to be Learned: Simultaneous Flexion, Adduction, and Inward rotation (Text Box 206)

1. Goal of exercise: • have nervous system learn and/or reinforce flexion • have nervous system learn and/or reinforce adduction, inward rotation • develop strength of trunk for stability during academic activity • develop more efficient reaction time • improve convergence of eyes 2. What is needed: • mat or smooth padded surface • two wooden blocks to make sound (or sudden loud clap of hands)	3. The environment: • quiet, dimly lit room • a sudden loud sound at the proper time 4. Position of the child: • on back with forearms on chest, fingers loosely flexed • hips and knees flexed • feet flat on floor 5. Number of repetitions: • minimum of five times 6. How many times day/week: • 3 times a week • more is better, benefit never ends

In a dimly lit room, the child gets into the Quick Tuck starting position by placing himself on his back on a mat or similar surface to protect his spine, with forearms on his chest, knees bent, and feet flat on the floor. He keeps his forearms (crossed or uncrossed) held securely on his chest, with his fingers loosely flexed, knees and feet held together (legs are not crossed) and his eyes closed.

Starting Position   Quick Tuck (Ed Snapp)

The adult then tells the child to tuck into a tight ball by raising his legs to his chest and by raising his head to his knees. If child cannot raise his legs to his chest and raise his head to his knees, proceed to #2. Quick Tucks with Support. See below.

If the child demonstrates he can make these movements the adult then tells him to "Relax." She then says to the child, "When you hear this sound (adult claps her hands together or strikes the wooden blocks together), this is the signal for you to tuck into a tight ball as quickly as possible. Keep your eye lids closed while looking toward your belly button." The child, with his eyes closed, waits for the Quick Tuck signal.

> **NOTE:** Your child may be able to move into a tightly tucked position but cannot hold this position for any length of time before putting his head and/or feet down or losing his balance and falling over to one side. Your child may benefit by doing Quick Tucks with Support until he has the ability to hold the Quick Tuck position without support for five seconds.

The child responds to the sudden, loud sound by quickly and simultaneously pulling every part of his body into a tight ball. He keeps his knees, legs, and feet together. Ankles are flexed and arms remain against chest. He should try to have his knees as close to his chest as possible. The head, neck and the upper and lower trunk will be raised from the floor. The adult silently counts up to five seconds, and then cues the child to relax by saying "Relax." The child relaxes so as to return to the starting position and silently waits (five to ten seconds) for the sound to be repeated. The entire sequence is repeated a minimum of five times.

The five to ten seconds relaxation phase is just as important as the active phase.

44

Starting Position

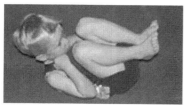

Quick Tuck

Relax (Starting Position)

2. Quick Tucks with Support (1D)

When a child is unable to perform the Quick Tucks use the Quick Tucks with Support. If he is unable to either raise the upper parts of his body off the mat or the lower parts of his body to be above his trunk, then giving support is appropriate. The child will also **need more** of the flexed position activity. (See page 25 for Flexion Positioning).

In a dimly lit room, the child lies on his back on a mat or similar surface to protect his spine. His head is supported in flexion with a high pillow and the flexed hips are three to four inches from a wall with knees flexed and the bottom of his feet resting on the wall. Forearms are held securely on chest and may be crossed or uncrossed, fingers are loosely flexed, knees and feet held together (legs are not crossed). Eyes should be looking at the belly button area.

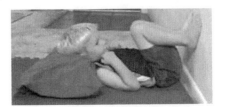
Ready Position

Tuck

Relax (Starting Position)

The adult says to the child, "When you hear this sound (adult claps her hands together or strikes the wooden blocks together), this is the signal for you to tuck into a tight ball as quickly as possible. Keep your eye lids closed and look toward your belly button." The child with his eyes closed waits for the Quick Tuck signal.

The child responds to the sudden, loud sound by quickly and simultaneously pulling every part of his body into a tight ball. He keeps his knees, legs, and feet together as they move toward his upper body. Ankles are flexed. Arms remain against the chest as the upper body moves toward his belly button. He should try to have his knees as close to his chest as possible and his head as close to his knees as possible. The adult silently counts five seconds, and then cues the child to relax by saying, "Relax." The child returns to the starting position and silently waits (five to ten seconds) for the sound. Repeat the entire sequence a minimum of five times. Vary the length of relaxation so that the signal or sound elicits a startle response.

The five to ten seconds relaxation phase is just as important as the active phase.

NOTE: Always include Startle Extension activity after any Flexion activity. (See page 50 for Startle Extension).

46

E. Extension

1. Tuck and Kick-out (1D)

Concept to be Learned: Quickly Moving from Prenatal Flexion to Prenatal Extension (Text Box 207)

1. Goal of exercise:
  • develop/reinforce ability to change from flexion to extension of trunk and legs
  • develop/reinforce ability to change from adduction and inward rotation to abduction and outward rotation of the forearms and shoulders
2. What is needed:
  • mat or smooth padded surface
  • two wooden blocks to make sounds, (or sudden loud clap of hands)
	3. The environment:
	  • quiet, dimly lit room
	  • a sudden loud sound at the proper times
	4. Position of the child:
	  • on back, forearms on chest
	  • hips and knees flexed
	  • feet flat on floor
	5. Number of repetitions:
	  • minimum of five times
	6. How many times day/week:
	  • 3 times a week
	  • more is better,
	  • benefit never ends

The child must be able to do the Quick Tucks Without Support before doing the Tuck and Kick-out.

The environment, starting position, and signal are the same as that of the Quick Tucks. In a dimly lit room, the child lies on his back on a mat or similar surface to protect his spine. Forearms are held securely on chest and may be crossed or uncrossed, fingers are loosely flexed. The hips and knees are flexed with feet flat on the floor. The knees and feet are held together (legs are not crossed).

The child will respond to two loud sounds, about five-seconds apart. All counting is to be silent.

47

Rest   Tuck   Kick-out (Ed Snapp)

Say to the child, "When you hear this sound (make the sound), tuck into a tight ball as quickly as possible and hold. When you hear the sound again (make the sound again), simultaneously kick legs out and rotate the flexed arms to the side and hold until I say, 'relax'," the child returns to the starting position.

The adult silently counts five seconds after each sound cue. Wait five to ten seconds after the relax cue, and then repeat the entire sequence.

The five to ten seconds relaxation phase is just as important as the active phase.

Observe the child for the following:
On the first sound the child instantly forms the tight ball in a flexed position and holds it tightly for five seconds.

On the second sound the child instantly kicks his legs out as the arms rotate to the side while the head and upper back remain off the mat. He holds this position for five seconds.

On the verbal cue "Relax" the child relaxes and returns to the starting position. The adult silently waits five to ten seconds before giving the next cue. After the five to ten seconds relaxation period, repeat a maximum of five times.

The five to ten seconds relaxation phase is just as important as the active phase.

48

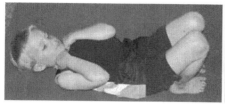
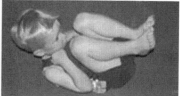

Rest   Tuck

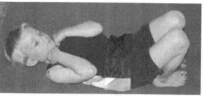

Kick-out   Relax (Starting Position)

The child responds:

> On the first sound: The child responds to the first sudden, loud sound by quickly and simultaneously flexing, adducting, and inwardly rotating every part of his body into a tight ball. He keeps his knees, legs, and feet together. Hips, knees, and ankles are flexed and arms remain against chest as he flexes the upper part of his body. He should try to have his knees as close to his chest as possible and his head as close to his knees as possible. The child holds the tight ball position for up to five seconds. The adult silently counts five seconds, and then cues the second sound.

> On the second sound: The child simultaneously kicks his legs out. His legs should be extended and held up off the mat. The shoulders are outwardly rotated, which brings the arms away from his body (with elbows bent) out to his side. The upper body, elbows and hands remain flexed. This places the hands at approximately shoulder level. The head and chest remain slightly forward, off the mat.

The adult silently counts five seconds, and then cues the child to relax by saying "Relax." The child returns to the starting position. Wait five to ten seconds then repeat the entire sequence a maximum of five times or as limited by fatigue.

The five to ten seconds relaxation phase is just as important as the active phase.

2. Startle Extension (1D)

Concept to be Learned: Coordinating Upper Gaze with Trunk Extension (Text Box 208)

---

1. Goal of exercise:
    - full extension of neck, trunk, hips, knees, ankles, fingers
    - develop ability to change from relaxation of trunk to extension abduction and outward rotation of the forearms and shoulders
    - build trunk stability for academic activity
    - coordinate upward vision with trunk extension
2. What is needed:
    - smooth, firm surface
    - two wooden blocks to make sounds (or sudden loud clap of hands)
    - a designated visual target

3. The environment:
    - quiet, dimly lit room
    - a sudden loud sound at proper times
4. Position of the child:
    - on stomach, on floor, face to one side
    - forearms inwardly rotated and near or under chest
    - top of feet on floor with big toes touching
5. Number of repetitions:
    - minimum of five times
6. How many times day/week:
    - 3 times a week
    - more is better,
    - benefit never ends

The adult demonstrates by lying prone on the floor with flexed arms and loosely fisted hands under her chest. The head is turned to one side and legs extended with big toes touching. She then rapidly and simultaneously lifts and extends her upper trunk and neck and moves her flexed arms

50

out to the side with open hands at shoulder level. Her head is forward and upward with eyes looking at a designated target. The target should be 8 feet or more straight ahead of her, 3 inches or more in diameter, and about three feet above the floor. A doorknob would work well as the target.

In a dimly lit room, the child is on his stomach on the floor. This activity does not need to be on a cushioned surface because there is no pressure on the backbone.

This activity is demonstrated to the child, and then performed by the child when the sound cue is heard. If some part of his position is not correct before the activity, gently and silently move his body to the correct position. If his position is incorrect during the extension phase, make a mental note and demonstrate the activity to the child again.

The child's head is turned to one side and his arms are flexed, adducted, and inwardly rotated under his chest with flexed elbows and fingers. His legs are extended and remain on the floor with hips inwardly rotated, with ankles extended and the **top of the feet in contact with the floor.** Legs and feet are together with big toes touching. After the signal when the child is fully extended his eyes are open looking upward at the designated target. His body is aligned with his head so that he can be looking ahead at the target.

Start on Stomach   Startle Extension

Relax (Starting Position)

Say to the child, "When you hear this loud sound (make the sound), extend **very quickly** by lifting your head, arms, elbows, and chest off the floor. Open your hands out to the side like this and look at the (designated target)."

As the child responds to the sound signal, look for lifted head pointed straight ahead, with shoulders and chest off the floor, elbows flexed with arms lifted to the side, fingers spread. If the child still has his head turned to the side, tell him to look at the (designated target) in front of him. Feet can remain on the floor or be lifted slightly. The adult silently counts five seconds, and then cues the child to relax by saying "Relax."

After the child relaxes, the head is turned to the opposite side so the other side of the face is in contact with the surface to start the next extension. This encourages equal strength to develop on both sides of the body.

The child returns to the starting position and silently waits five to ten seconds then repeats the entire sequence as cued for a maximum of five times or as limited by the child's fatigue.

NOTE: The child should raise his head, shoulders and chest off the floor by contracting the muscles of the back and neck, not from using his hands and arms as in a push-up. **Always include Startle Extension activity after Flexion activity.**

The five to ten seconds relaxation phase is just as important as the active phases.

F. Rotation and Sequencing of Arms and Legs (1D)

These rotational and sequential exercises, built upon the prenatal release of flexion, adduction, and inward rotation, lead up to crawling. The body surfaces that were sensitized by Light Touch activities are the body parts that will learn to move the body across a surface.

52

A slick, hard, smooth surface without texture makes a great crawling surface. (See page 23 for crawling surface) This slick surface allows movement across it with as little resistance as possible. Keep the crawling surface clean and free from any dust and/or debris that might take away from the smoothness of the surface. Sweatpants and top or a short-sleeved shirt and shorts would be appropriate attire. A face cloth may be used to keep the face clean and in contact with the surface.

Concept to be Learned: Rotation and Sequencing of Arms and Legs (Text Box 209)

1. Goal of exercise:
   - develop movement sequence used in crawling patterns
   - develop inward rotation required for applying pressure to the floor for crawling
   - develop overall coordination required for reading, writing, sports
   - stimulate and integrate both sides of the brain for learning
2. What is needed:
   - firm smooth slick surface
   - optional: face cloth or ski mask may be used to protect the face from surface
3. The environment:
   - quiet, dimly lit room
4. Position of the child:
   - lying on stomach, face turned to working limb, hands rotated in under the chest, fingers flexed
   - shoulders relaxed, legs rotated inward, big toes touching
5. Number of repetitions:
   Arms: (refer to figure on Rotation Sequence of the Arms, page 54)
   - For the arms repeat (a), then (b) for several days until proficient, then (c) 4 to 6 times
   Legs: (refer to figure on Rotation Sequence of the legs, page 56)
   - For the legs repeat (a), then (b), then (c) until proficient, then (d) 4 to 6 times
6. How many times day/week:
   - 3 times a week
   - more is better,
   - benefit never ends

At first, each segment of the complete movement of the arms is performed, learned, and understood separately. Then the entire sequence is performed, learned, and understood as a whole. Similar sequence is done for the legs: each segment is performed, learned and understood separately; then the entire sequence of the legs is performed, learned, and understood as a whole.

The adult demonstrates the position and movement to the child. If part of the position is not correct when the child does it, silently and gently move the body into the correct position.

1. Rotation Sequence of the Arms (1D)

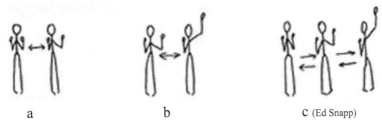

a   b   c (Ed Snapp)

    a. Inward/outward rotation of arm:
The child is lying on his stomach, face turned to the right side, toes pointed inward, and hands rotated in and held under his chest with his shoulders relaxed. The legs are rotated inwardly with big toes touching. A face cloth may be used to keep the face clean and in contact with the surface. The eyes watch the moving hand as the right arm rotates out to the side, elbow still flexed, forearm parallel to the body. He relaxes the shoulder. The inner side of the hand (palm) and the inner side of the forearm are resting on the surface. He then rotates the flexed arm inward and slides it back under the chest, and relaxes the shoulder to return to the starting position.

If the child does not relax the shoulder when the adult says "Relax," the adult may gently press the shoulder down to the floor each time until the child is able to relax

54

on his own. The child needs more integration of the light touch sensation.

The adult may say "out" or "in" as necessary. Repeat the out—in sequence 4 to 6 times, relaxing after each movement.

The relaxation phases are just as important as the active phase.

b. Arm extension:
Start with the right arm out, elbow flexed, and the shoulder relaxed. The child's eyes are to be focused on his hand, which is flat on the floor, as the hand slides upward above his head as a result of the elbow and shoulder extension. The forearm and palm are kept in a line parallel to the body and in contact with the floor. He continues to watch his hand all the way up, relax, watch his hand all the way down, and relax. Up while watching, relax, down while watching, relax. Repeat the up—down sequence 4 to 6 times. The inner forearm and palm should be flat on the floor at all times. After the final slide up and down, rotate the arm back under the chest and relax.

The relaxation phases are just as important as the active phases.

If the adult observes that the child does not move his eyes appropriately to track the hand while the arm is moving, without comment press on the child's hand as a non-verbal cue.

c. Full sequence:
From the same position as in a. above, with the arm under the chest, rotate the right arm out, relax, up, relax, down, relax, in, relax. Eyes should be watching the moving hand at all times. Repeat 4 to 6 times. If necessary use the cue words: "out—up—down—in".

Turn face to the left side and repeat the entire sequence (a, b, and c) using the left arm.

2. Rotation Sequence of the Legs (1D)

   Take time to fully develop ALL of the following individual movements of the lower limbs, for these individual movements are the foundation of crawling.

(Ed Snapp) [2.5]

Before beginning the Rotation Sequences of the Legs, vigorously rub the top of the foot, the inner surface of the heel, and the inner surface of the ankle of the working leg to sensitize the skin. This increased awareness of sensation will aid in keeping the top of the foot and the front of the ankle in contact with the surface of the floor. When the ankle is fully released from flexion and fully extended, the top of the foot will be against the floor.

If the child is observed to completely roll his trunk over to the other side when trying to rotate the working leg outward, he needs more light touch sensations to bring about the full release of hip flexion.

a. Rotation of foot:
   The child is lying on his stomach, his face turned to the right side (the same side as the leg which is being moved), the feet and toes are turned inward, with big toes touching, and hands are rotated in and held under his chest. **The front of the body remains in contact with the floor** as he outwardly rotates the right hip to turn the right foot from inward and downward to outward and downward. Make

56

sure that the top of the foot slides across the floor and that the inner side of the heel is in contact with the floor at the end of the outward/downward phase. Relax in this position, then rotate foot back in, sliding the top of the foot against the floor once again to resume starting position.

Repeat rotating the foot out, relax, back in and relax, keeping the ankle extended at all times. Repeat this sequence 4 to 6 times. Repeat this exercise with the other foot.

If the child is not keeping his trunk and pelvis in contact with the floor, he has not developed full release of flexion, and needs to experience more flexion activities or more of the light touch developmental activities. He may also need the cue "relax" after he has turned the ankle outward, or has raised the knee.

The adult may say "out" or "in" as necessary.

b. Flexion and extension of ankle:
Start with the right foot out and down, with inner side of the heel, trunk and pelvis in contact with the surface. Flex the ankle up, keeping the heel in contact with the floor, relax; straighten and extend the ankle to allow the foot to point out and down, relax. Repeat this up—down sequence of the foot 4 to 6 times.

It may be necessary for the adult to hold the heel down on the surface during this sequence and say, "up—relax" and/or "down—relax," as necessary until the child can perform without the cues.

Repeat this up—down sequence 4 to 6 times, relaxing after each movement. Repeat this exercise with the other foot.

The relaxation is just as important as the active part of the movement.

If the child rolls his trunk and lifts his pelvis from the floor during this movement he needs more emphasis on light touch and more time for the relaxation phase before continuing.

c. Flexion of hip and knee:
    Start with ankle flexed, hip rotated outwardly, and hip and knee extended. The hip and knee flex as the leg is raised as high as possible (at or above 90 degrees flexion). The ankle remains flexed with the heel in contact with the floor. The child relaxes his body in this position. He then extends his leg (leading with his heel), pushes his foot back down, gradually straightening his knee as his leg moves down, and then relaxes. The hip remains outwardly rotated and the ankle remains flexed, with inner heel in contact with the floor.

    The lower leg remains parallel to the body during all of the upward and downward movement. The knee, lower leg and the inside of the foot, including the heel, slide in contact with the floor during the hip and knee movements. If necessary use the cue words, "up—down" until the child can perform without the cues.

    Repeat the up, down sequence of the hip and knee 4 to 6 times, relaxing in between movements. Repeat this exercise with the other hip and knee.

d. Full sequence:
    The full sequence combines the movements from a, b, and c. From the starting position of a, the child rotates his hip and his foot out then flexes the ankle up while keeping his heel in contact with the floor. He flexes his hip and knee up to approximately 90 degrees, and then leads with his heel as he pushes his foot back down by straightening his hip and knee. He extends his ankle so the foot is pointing downward, and then rotates the hip, leg, and ankle inward to have the big toes of the

58

feet touching. One entire sequence is completed before relaxing. If necessary use the cue words, "out—flex—up—down—in—relax" until the child can perform without the cues.

Repeat this sequence 4 to 6 times.

Turn face to the left side and repeat the rotation and flexions separately (a, b, and c) as you did for the right side, followed by the full sequence (d).

Take time to fully develop ALL of the above individual movements of the lower limbs, for these individual movements are the foundation of crawling.

G. Crawling (2D/3D)

All developmental exercises presented and discussed so far are purposeful and serve as the background in preparation for a child's mobility (moving across a surface.) For example, alternating leg movements developed prenatally during light touch leg rubs are the same type of alternating movements used later when one leg alternates with the other leg for crawling, creeping, and walking.

The mechanics of these mobility patterns are in our genetic code. The correct sequence for mobility patterns of crawling is: the Basic Crawl, the Homolateral Crawl, and the Cross Pattern Crawl. The next pattern of mobility is Creeping on hands and knees. Creeping is followed by pulling up into the upright position for walking, first sideways around furniture then by walking forward.

The Basic Crawl integrates the head and upper body with the lower extremities. When crawling the child is not building background but rather integrating and refining the background he has already developed and understands. If the child has several background errors he may not be benefiting by the crawling patterns. He needs to revisit the background to experience again the developmental sensations and movements (light touch sensations, flexion positioning, quick tucks, extension). It would be a good practice to revisit the earlier (basic) developmental program periodically to build more background, then bring the program back up to the higher level activity of crawling to again integrate newly acquired additional background into one's coordination.

Crawling develops strength, endurance, and sensory abilities. Crawling also develops coordination of the eyes as they track the working hand on the side to which the head is turned. When a child fixes both eyes on the object and crawls to it, his eyes must converge a little more because the viewing distance becomes shorter. It is this moving through space and the converging of his eyes as he glances up to see the object that helps build his understanding of far point distance/dimension. [2-6]

Movement is controlled by sensory input. Do not tell a child to come to you in crawling and do not tell him to crawl to an object because being involved in higher cortical awareness level prevents him from learning from the sensations of his own movements. Sensations he learns from correct crawling patterns prepare the child to better understand and coordinate his movements for creeping, walking, and lifetime activities. Individuals with well-developed sensations enjoy highly coordinated movements and often are those individuals who excel in sports.

The description that follows details the patterns for crawling; these details are included to enable the adult to recognize a fully developed pattern. These details should not be used to continually give verbal instructions or to constantly correct the child as he moves. Continuous verbal instructions and corrections are distractions that interfere with the child's ability to internalize sensations he should learn from crawling. If the child is not doing the crawls correctly go back to previous developmental exercises, such as rotational sequencing of the arms and legs, and/or light touch leg and arm rubs, and/or deep pressure stimulation.

The adult may occasionally correct the child by touching or repositioning the body part that needs to be corrected. For example, if the child pushes with his toes instead of with the inside of the foot, gently move the foot into the correct position. Snapp emphasized that when a child is ready, a gentle correction is all that is needed.

If the child is in need of correction in more than one body part, gently move only one body part into correct position as he moves across the floor. When the body retains the first correction, then another body part can be gently moved into the correct position. If the body part does not retain the gentle correction, then the child needs to experience more of earlier steps leading up to crawling. Children who have the correct crawling pattern from the beginning will still benefit from crawling. Crawling integrates earlier developmental movement patterns and coordinates the movements of the shoulders and hips.

Children become quite proficient in crawling. As their proficiency increases it is expected that their rate of movement across the surface will also increase. Crawling fast is acceptable as long as a child maintains correct movements and he is not racing against someone or against time.

It is important to not teach crawling step by step, but to let the child's body organize the pattern on its own.

Concept to be Learned: Integration of Vision and Developmental Movements (Text Box 210)

1. Goal of exercise:
  • develop coordination and strength to propel the body forward
  • enhance eye-hand coordination needed for reading, writing, sports
  • stimulate and integrate both sides of the brain for learning
2. What is needed:
  • hard smooth slick surface
  • optional: face cloth or ski mask to protect face from floor surface
3. The environment:
  • quiet, dimly lit room
  • slick smooth surface without texture with length of at least 18 feet
  • shorts or sweatpants and top or bare arms
	4. Position of the child:
	  • <u>Starting position</u>: on stomach face turned to the side of working leg
	  • elbows flexed with open hands about shoulder level
	  • legs rotated inward
	  • big toes touching
	5. Number of repetitions:
	  • best if done 100 feet or more if possible
	6. How many times day/week:
	  • 3 times a week
	  • more is better,
	  • benefit never ends

Crawling is to be done in a quiet, dimly lit room on a slick, hard, smooth surface without texture. (See page 23 for crawling surface) This slick surface allows movement across it with as little resistance as possible. Sweatpants or shorts and a short sleeved shirt would be appropriate attire. A winter ski-type hat/mask may be used over the face to protect it from any irritation from the surface.

1. Basic Crawl: (2D)

The Basic Crawl Sequence (Ed Snapp—adapted 2011) (2-5)

Starting Position: The child lies on his stomach with his head turned to the right. The palms are flat and slightly above shoulder level, with elbows flat on the floor. The straight legs are resting on the floor with the big toes touching. Bringing the toes together at the end of the movement is the developmental background for walking and running with hips, knees and ankles in alignment.

NOTE: When the child was on his belly on the floor, Snapp would instruct the child to "Move across the floor as best you can".

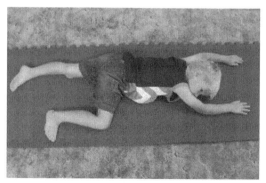

Start of the Basic Crawl

Movement begins as the right hip rotates outwardly, the right foot also rotates outwardly and the ankle flexes. The right lower extremity slides upward so as to have the right hip, knee and ankle bent at least 90 degrees. Both arms slide forward with the palms flat on the floor and elbows slightly bent. The trunk, inner knee, inner side of foot, inner side of arms, palms of the hands, and side of the face maintain contact with the floor as they are moved across the surface.

The child keeps his hands and right foot in place and presses and pulls with both arms as he pushes against the floor with the inner side of the knee and foot to slide his body forward. After completion of the forward motion the legs will be inwardly rotated with the big toes touching and the front surfaces of the legs in contact with the floor as the ankles are extended.

The child then turns his head to the left and repeats the motions with the left leg and both arms. The child continues the Basic Crawl across the floor by using this series of movements. The correct Basic Crawl is a fluid motion where a leg and both arms move at the same time.

It is best when the crawling is done 100 feet or more. The child may, however, need to work up to this distance. The longer the crawling surface the better, because there will be fewer interruptions from the turns.

If the child rolls over to the other side of the pelvis to slide the right leg upward it is an indication that the nervous system has not yet learned to release flexion, adduction, and inward rotation. It is the complete release of flexion, adduction, and inward rotation that allows the hip to be relaxed and the pelvic area of the trunk to be flat on the floor. More developmental background work (light touch, leg rubs, and pressure to name a few) in associated environments will be required.

2. Homolateral Crawl: (2D)

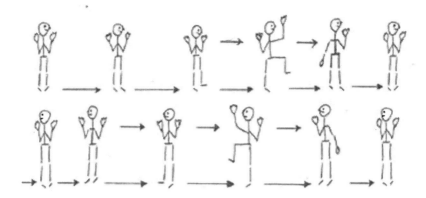

Homolateral Crawl Sequence (Ed Snapp—adapted 2011) [2-5]

At least a few weeks of doing Basic Crawl is necessary for the child to develop the proper integration of the upper and lower extremities. As the child becomes visually aware of his hand movements on the side he is facing, he will progress into the next sequence of crawling, which is the Homolateral Crawl.

When this transition occurs his crawling time should now include part of the distance in Basic Crawl and part of the distance in Homolateral Crawl. Later, when the Cross Pattern Crawl is a part of the child's movement, the three crawling patterns will be incorporated into the crawling time as described below.

The Homolateral Crawl uses a similar sequence of arm and leg movements as those used in Basic Crawling. But for Homolateral Crawl only one upper extremity (one arm) moves with the same side lower extremity (one leg). Moving the arm and leg on the same side at the same time is what makes this movement homolateral.

Homolateral crawling is not taught. When the child is ready, he will move into this pattern. You may, however suggest to the child that he move forward only the arm and leg on the side he is facing. He pulls down with the arm and pushes with the leg to move the body forward. The eyes follow the working hand and keep watching that hand as he propels his body forward until his shoulders are even with the hand that remains in place. Because the child is watching the hand on the side that he is facing his neck flexes to allow the eyes to look downward at the hand that ends up near shoulder level. Homolateral Crawling is associated with peripheral vision because vision is attached to the working hand located to the side of the child.

Next, he turns his head to the other side and repeats the motion with the arm and leg on that side. The eyes follow the working hand. It is through this pattern that vision becomes coordinated with the hand and will remain so throughout the Cross Pattern Crawl, which is the next developmental movement.

The correct Homolateral Crawl is a fluid motion where the right leg and right arm move at the same time. Sometimes a child who has not yet completely integrated the Homolateral Crawl will briefly return to the Basic Crawl after he makes a turn to go back across the crawling surface. If, after a few strokes, he does not return to Homolateral Crawl after he makes his turn at the end of a lap, gently press on the hand that is to remain in place. If this does not remind him to keep one hand in place, then say to him, "Move only the hand you are watching."

As with the Basic Crawl it is best to do the Homolateral Crawl 100 feet or more.

The Homolateral Crawl integrates the upper right side with the lower right side, the upper left side with the lower left side, and hooks up eye—hand correlation. The two sides of the body need to develop independently of each other. However, the Homolateral Crawl DOES NOT promote the integration of the two sides of the body together. It will be important to work on the Homolateral Crawl for a relatively brief period (1-2 weeks) only and then move on to the Cross Pattern Crawl to promote the integration of the two sides of the body. The Cross Pattern Crawl is described below.

3. Cross Pattern Crawl (3D)

Cross Pattern Crawl Sequence (Ed Snapp—adapted 2011) [2-5]

After a few weeks the child should develop the necessary integration of the upper and lower extremities by doing Homolateral Crawl. As the pattern of the Homolateral Crawl is integrated the child will progress into the next sequence of crawling that is the Cross Pattern Crawl. The Cross Pattern Crawl integrates both sides of the body together. When this transition occurs his crawling time should combine the patterns together—part of the distance in Basic Crawl, part of the distance in Homolateral Crawl, and part of the distance in Cross Pattern Crawl.

The Cross Pattern Crawl is not taught. When the child is ready, he will move into this pattern. You may suggest to the child that he do the Cross Pattern Crawl by moving the arm on the side he is facing (right side) and the opposite leg (left) forward. Then he simultaneously pushes into the floor with his hand and arm as he straightens his leg while the leg and inner side of the foot push into the floor. It is this coordinated action that propels his body across the surface. The eyes follow the working hand. Next, he turns his head to the other side and moves the left arm and right leg forward. Then he pushes into the floor with his hand and arm as he straightens the leg while the leg and inner side of the foot push into the floor to move the body forward. The eyes follow the working hand. Continuing in this pattern is Cross Pattern Crawling.

The correct Cross Pattern Crawl is a fluid motion where one leg and the opposite arm move at the same time.

As with all crawling patterns it is best when the Cross Pattern Crawl is done 100 feet or more. After a few weeks of Cross Pattern Crawling the light level may be increased to normal lighting.

Snapp often combined the patterns together—i.e., Basic first, then Basic and Homolateral. He may have done Homolateral for only a week or two before switching to Homolateral and Cross Pattern. At other times he may have combined Basic, Homolateral, Cross Pattern, then switched to only Cross Pattern.

During Snapp's 1982 Pflugerville course a teacher asked him if it was alright to just do the crawling movements without actually crawling. He replied that the **movements themselves** would be helpful because the movement patterns are a part of the developmental complex and part of the environmental complex **but would never complete the developmental process.** He went on to say that he thought that **the forward movement is necessary because the loading of the muscles changes** with each forward movement. Snapp continued the answer by saying that there was no way someone could be accurate on the muscle loading during the forward movement by just sliding the hands back and forth, so the forward movement is necessary.

H. Creeping (3D)

As an infant begins to lift himself off the floor onto his hands and knees he will start rocking back and forth on his hands and knees. The hands are flat on the floor with the front of the lower leg and top of the feet remain in contact with the floor. When he feels confident in his strength and coordination he will begin Creeping. Creeping is done in normal lighting.

The description for Creeping is included to enable the adult to recognize a fully developed pattern. The description should not to be used to continually give verbal instructions or to constantly correct the child as he moves.

The child's body is supported on the palms of the hands and the knees with the front of the lower legs and the top of the feet in contact with the surface as the leg moves forward. The palms of the hands and fingers are flat on the surface with the fingers pointing forward. The head is up, allowing the child to view his environment.

Creeping is done in cross pattern fashion. The right hand and left knee simultaneously move forward and, as he takes the weight on his hand and knee, the body continues to move forward. Then the left hand and right knee simultaneously move forward and he continues in this pattern. The tops of the feet always maintain contact with the surface. The forward movement of the hands and the knees should be in a straight line.

In the correct Creeping pattern, the hands and knees contact the floor simultaneously. Since the hand and knee contact the floor simultaneously there should be only a single sound as the floor is contacted. If more than one contact sound is heard, the limbs are not being moved simultaneously. The hips remains stable, not dropping side to side as the weight switches from one knee to the other. The palms and fingers are flat on the floor. If the child is not Creeping correctly, go back to previous developmental exercises such as Crawling, Rotational Sequencing of the Arms and Legs, and/or Light Touch Leg and Arm Rubs, and/or Deep Pressure Stimulation. It may be more comfortable for the older child (compared to an infant) if Creeping can be done on a softer surface such as a mat or a vinyl over a carpet.

Snapp spoke of how an infant moves across the floor in order to reach or touch some object a distance from him. The child reaches his extended arm and hand to get the object, but since he has not yet gone far enough, he goes a bit more and reaches out again for the object. This may be repeated several times before he either touches the object or has the hand go beyond it where he can draw the object to himself. Creeping and the activity of reaching for an object aids in the development of depth perception. The child initiating his own Creeping and reaching for an object is within the developmental sequence. Requesting a child to go to an object takes Creeping out of the developmental sequence.

Though Creeping is not a developmental exercise, it enhances coordination and strength. It is also important in stimulating and integrating both sides of the brain for learning. Creeping is also a link in the developmental process from Crawling to pulling to a stand to cruise sideways with hands on the walls or holding on to furniture to taking independent steps.

Observe your child's Creeping and watch for Cross Pattern movements, proper placement of hands and knees, and hip stability. Return to Crawling if the child is not Creeping in Cross Pattern, is not placing hands and knees properly, or if his hip is unstable.

I. Walking (3D)

The first walking pattern is the "toddler's walk". In this pattern the child takes his full weight on one side then shifts his weight to the other side in homolateral fashion. In time a cross pattern walk develops with the arms and legs working in opposition to one another.

Apparently, all of the tracts that are put together by physical movements are the same tracts and follow the same sequencing as the tracts for classroom learning. When the child learns movements, you're setting the child up for good classroom learning. When there is any deviation from the control of these particular tract movements, then we have difficulties in the classroom. Ed Snapp [2-7]

References

2-1. Boyd, Margie, *Different—The Boy Who Couldn't Write*, Rockcrest Press, Georgetown, Texas, 2008, p 101.

2-2. Snapp, Edward A., Jr., P.T., Developmental Learning, unpublished paper, 2002 made available by Ed's daughter, Susan Snapp.

2-3. Small, Roxanne, P. T., *Building Babies Better, Developing a Solid Foundation for Your Child*, Trafford Publishing, Victoria, BC, Canada, 2005, pp 49-51.

2-4. Snapp, Edward A., Jr., P.T., "Developmental Exercises", unpublished material Copyright 2002, made available by Ed's daughter, Susan Snapp.

2-5. Images adapted by Lucy Alff, 1982; Dr. Darlene Schmidt, 2011.

2-6. Snapp, Edward A., Jr., P.T., lecture notes, Pflugerville, Texas, 1979.

2-7. Snapp, Edward A., Jr., P.T., "Chronologically Controlled Developmental Education" presentation to Texas Association for Children With Learning Disabilities (TACLD), Austin, Texas, 1977.

VISUAL PERCEPTION

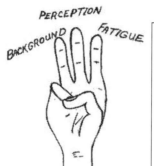

BACKGROUND: Stay within child's developmental and educational background.

PERCEPTION: Stay within child's perceptual level for each of his senses.

FATIGUE: Stop before fatigue of the nervous system is apparent.

<u>SNAPP Principle</u>: **Inaccurate perception of hearing, seeing, and other sensory input results in unintended responses. Perceptions can be enhanced with correct sensory and sensory motor activities.**

Ed Snapp in the Classroom

When observing in a classroom, Ed noticed that a child was coloring with his head practically on his paper. Aside to the teacher he asked "What's wrong with this child?" The teacher replied, "There is nothing wrong with that child." Ed asked, "Why is that child coloring with his head practically on his paper?" The teacher responded, "A lot of them do that." Then Ed explained, "The child is laying down his head to eliminate the vision of one eye so that he won't see double."

Children often put their head close to the paper or rest their face on their hand to avoid seeing double. The nervous system does not tolerate double vision, so it shuts down one eye.

73

Visual Information

In this Chapter, Visual Perception, the activities start with the most basic 1D (One Dimension) activities before progressing to more complex activities of 2D (Two Dimension) and 3D (Three Dimension). Each 1D activity should be completed at a minimum of 90% accuracy before moving into any 2D activities. The same criteria apply to moving from 2D activities into 3D activities. Completion of 1D activities at the minimum of 90% accuracy provides a good foundation to building a better learner. Completion of any activity at a greater percentage of accuracy provides an even greater foundation for your child to build upon to reach his potential. For more information on **SNAPP**'s Dimensions refer to **SNAPP**'s Dimensions on page 14 and to **SNAPP**'s Dimensions listed in the Glossary and/or Appendix A.

Initially the prenatal environment is darkness. Darkness is experienced before light. At birth the child is introduced to light and sees in natural light for the first time thus establishing the initial time and environment for the understanding of contrast between light and dark. He understands this difference if his pupils react to light when light is introduced into a dark room.

As the child begins to crawl (See Basic Crawl on page 63) across the floor on his stomach his eyes begin to track the extending arm thus aiding in the development of eye-hand coordination. When a baby begins reaching for an object he often misses the object. His hand falls between his eyes and the object. He will then crawl toward the object until it is grasped. Once grasped or drawn toward himself, he begins to understand the distance between his eyes and his hands thus establishing the initial time and environment of eye-hand coordination.

Visual perception does not develop in isolation from the rest of the body. Perception as well as posture, coordination, and academic ability—all—benefit by doing the developmental exercises described in this book.

In teaching, present real objects first. Allow the child to explore them with all of his senses, in an environment with no distractions. Then introduce known objects on **SNAPP** Silhouette Cards. (See Silhouette Cards on page 115.) Use objects with which the child is familiar, and are within his language base. For example, use ball, box, car, cup, tree, or table. To guarantee success in learning, the child must recognize objects before proceeding with more complex activities.

At this point the concept of color is introduced. First the child is taught the various colors of objects in the room. **SNAPP** Color Cards (See Color Cards on page 119) are designed with one side of the card in a solid color and the back side in solid white.

Procedure for Perceptual Development

Crawling on a slick, hard smooth surface helps to integrate eye-hand movements. Without the benefits of sufficient crawling there could be gaps in the understanding of visual and tactile sensations. The arms and shoulders, as well as other body parts, receive valuable developmental information that may be incomplete and inaccurate without the benefit of crawling. For example, poor handwriting technique is often caused by developmental gaps and not from lack of practicing handwriting.

If at anytime the child does not understand a concept or is unable to perform any of these activities, take him back to earlier developmental activities within his perceptual background.

Activities: Contrasting Dark and Light (1D)

Flashing light exercises help with awareness and understanding of the contrast between light and darkness. It also provides a background for understanding the contrast between black print on a white background. Light stimulation activities provide for the ability to develop contraction of the pupils.

If a child is unable to read Silhouette Cards (See Silhouette Cards on page 115) he may not have learned the contrast of light and dark and/or the pupils of his eyes may not be contracting sufficiently to read the Silhouette Cards. When a child is reading Silhouette Cards he is then ready to read word cards.

A dimly lit environment is used during some activities in order to keep the eyes relaxed, and to create a stronger input stimulation when the flashing light stimulation is used. Some of the activities done in a dimly lit environment are: movement patterns, Deep Pressure Stimulation, Quick Tucks, Eye-Hand Tracking exercises, Basic Crawling, Homolateral Crawling, or other activities such as telling stories to the child.

Equipment needed:

100 watt frosted white light bulb in an un-shaded adjustable lamp fixture with a silent switch attached.

A darkened environment.

Peripheral light stimulation is presented first to the child followed by light stimulation straight ahead. The environment for each of the following flashing light activities is to spend 1-2 minutes in a dimly lit (twilight) environment prior to the exercise. Then change the environment to a room that is completely dark and do the flashing light stimulation activities. After Flashing Light Stimulation spend 1-2 minutes in a dimly lit (twilight) environment doing any activity associated with a dim environment.

In this exercise as well as other exercises in this book, the suggested sitting position of the child is with legs crossed. However, if your child cannot sit cross-legged or needs to change his position, he may sit in a chair or on the floor in a position more comfortable to him.

Concept to be Learned: Contrast Dark and Light in Peripheral Vision Field (Text Box 301)

1. Goal of exercise:
   • stimulation of peripheral vision
   • awareness readiness for reading silhouettes and symbols
2. What is needed:
   • un-shaded 100 watt frosted white light bulb
   • stand for light bulb
   • silent switch
3. The environment:
   • silent, completely dark room
   • comfortable temperature
4. Position of the child:
   • sitting cross legged with light at 60 degrees from midline of face
   • **looking straight ahead**
   • light is at eye level
   • bulb 18" to 24" from child's face
5. Number of repetitions:
   • ten times flashing light to right (1 sec. on, 4 sec. off)
   • ten times flashing light to left (1 sec. on, 4 sec. off)
6. How many times day/week:
   • twice daily 3 times per week
   • unit **SNAPP** Silhouette Cards can be read

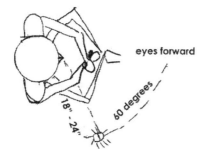

Peripheral Light Overhead View

Peripheral Light Front View

Peripheral Light Rear View

To stimulate the child's peripheral vision, he sits on the floor in a completely dark room. The light bulb is even with his eyes as he sits cross-legged, trunk erect, with the light 60 degrees from the midline of his face as illustrated above. He is not looking directly at the light but is looking forward. The light is at eye level and 18" to 24" from his face. He remains looking forward throughout the sequence of light-on and light-off as the adult uses the silent switch to turn the light **on for one second and off for four seconds.**

The silent switch is used so that the nervous system does not react to the sound of a switch indicating the lighting will change. The desired outcome by using the silent switch is that the nervous system is responding only to the changing of the illumination from darkness to light, or from light to darkness.

Repeat this peripheral light exercise ten times. The child then repositions himself so that the light is on his other side, 60 degrees from the midline of his face. Repeat this sequence of light-on and light-off ten times.

NOTE: Because this is a new concept it may be necessary to start out with only one flash of light on and light off. Your child may have to build up to ten on/off flashes of the light.

Concept to be Learned: Contrast of Dark and Light in Center Vision Field (Text Box 302)

1. Goal of exercise:
    - contrasting light and dark
    - readiness for reading silhouettes
2. What is needed:
    - un-shaded 100 watt frosted white light bulb
    - stand for light bulb
    - silent switch
3. The environment:
    - silent, dark or very dim room
    - comfortable temperature
4. Position of the child:
    - sitting cross legged on floor
    - 8 feet or more from light
    - light is at eye level
    - looking directly at the light
5. Number of repetitions:
    - ten cycles of 2 sec. on and 2 sec. off
6. How many times day/week:
    - twice daily 3 times per week
    - until SNAPP Silhouette Cards can be read

Light Straight Ahead

To stimulate awareness of the child's central vision, the child sits on the floor in a completely darkened room with legs crossed, trunk erect, facing the light that is at eye level and directly in front of him and **eight feet or more** from him. He remains

79

facing the light as the adult uses the silent switch (so that the child responds to light and not to the sound) to turn the light **on for two seconds and off for two seconds**. Repeat this sequence of light-on and light-off ten times.

Always do the two sets of light stimulation in the same session: Flashing Light to Each Side (peripheral) followed by Flashing Light Forward.

NOTE: Because this is a new concept it may be necessary to start out with only one flash of light on and light off. Your child may have to build up to more frequent flashes of the light.

Open Palm Tracing for Visual Development (2D)

Large Tracing Cards develop the background for visual perception, visual memory and for handwriting.

Equipment needed:
Large Tracing Cards with basic strokes used for writing printed letters
Lighted environment

1. Making the Cards (See Making the Cards in Appendix B)
Each **Tracing Card** contains a basic design. White poster boards measuring 14" x 28" are easily found in most grocery stores and are recommended for use as **Tracing Cards**. These poster boards can be cut in half so that **Tracing Cards** measure 14" x 14" or, for greater tracing length, 7" x 28". The design is made of a 2" wide black stroke, one basic stroke per card. These cards may be laminated to protect them from getting worn and/or tearing.

Concept to be Learned: Open Palm Tracing of Wide Black Line
(Text Box 303)

1. Goal of exercise:
  • visual perception
    development
  • visual memory
    development
  • handwriting
    development
  • readiness for reading
2. What is needed:
  • Basic Stroke Large
    Tracing Cards
3. The environment:
  • lighted room
	4. Position of the child:
	  • sitting crossed legged
	    on floor
	  • tracing card on the floor
	    in front of child
	5. Number of repetitions:
	  • 10 times back and forth
	    each hand per card
	6. How many times day/week:
	  • 3 times per week
	  • more is better, benefit
	    never ends

Tracing Position

2. Procedures for Tracing on the Large Tracing Cards
The child sits on the floor with legs crossed, trunk straight
while leaning as far forward as required for the palm of the
hand to reach the line being traced. The Tracing Card is
placed in front of the child.

The adult demonstrates to the child how to appropriately cover the eye and trace the stroke on the tracing card by placing her right palm on the Tracing Card and moving her hand left to right and then right to left. While demonstrating how to trace the stroke, she tells him, "I am not raising my hand from the card and I am watching my moving hand." At the end of the demonstration she tells the child, "Now you do it."

The child covers his left eye with his left hand. Care should be taken to place the fingers on the forehead and cup the palm over the eye to eliminate any pressure on the eye.

He places the flat palm of his right hand on the left side of the basic stroke and traces it. The fingers of his right hand are straight and lifted from the surface so that more sensation is concentrated on the palm of the hand. He moves his hand as required for the design, starting at the left side of the stroke. The child traces the stroke in both directions, left to right and then right to left, without raising his hand. **He is to keep looking at his tracing hand while tracing.** Repeat 10 times.

Now have the child trace the designs in both directions with his left hand, while covering his right eye. **He is to keep looking at his tracing hand while tracing.** Repeat 10 times.

Adult demonstrates again, this time with both eyes open. One hand is used to trace the design and the other hand is used to stabilize the Tracing Card. She comments to the child, "I am watching my moving hand." At the end of the demonstration, she tells the child, "Now you do it."

Watch his eye to be sure he is looking at his hand as it moves across the design. If he is not looking at his hand, apply light pressure to the moving hand to draw attention to his tracing hand.

The child then traces the basic stroke 10 times in both directions with **both eyes open** using one hand, then using the other hand. **He is to keep looking at his tracing hand while tracing.** He traces each of the basic strokes on the Tracing Cards using the same procedure.

It is not necessary to trace all of the basic strokes at one setting, but the above tracing sequence is done for each of the Tracing Cards described below.

The adult watches to ensure that the palm of the child's hand, not his fingers, is being used to trace the design. Change to another activity before the child becomes fatigued.

3. Tracing Cards
   The Tracing Cards are used to develop large (gross) motor control of the shoulders and trunk. The palm of the hand is used to trace the design. Make sure the whole palm, rather than the fingers, is in contact with the design on the Tracing Card.

   The Tracing Cards are always presented in a specific sequence, but no more than two or three cards are introduced in a day. A new card is not presented until the child can successfully watch his moving hand while tracing the current shape. According to Snapp vertical lines are most easily understood, then horizontal lines, and then circles. The Vertical Line card is presented first to the child, next the Horizontal Line Card and then the Circle Card is presented.

   When tracing the following designs, the child is to trace in both directions (down and up, left and right, counterclockwise and clockwise). Repeat each design several times before moving on to the next Card. After tracing with one palm, the child then traces with the other palm.

   Present the Tracing Cards in the sequence and procedure described.

a) Vertical Line

To trace a vertical line, place palm at the top of the line and slide the palm to the bottom of the line, then retrace back to the starting point. Repeat several times with one palm then the other palm.

b) Horizontal Line

To trace a horizontal line, place palm at the left end of the line and slide the palm to the right end of the line, then retrace back to the starting point. Repeat several times with one palm then the other palm.

c) Circle

To trace a circle, place the child's palm at 2:00 o'clock, then trace counterclockwise completely around the circle. Then place the child's palm at 10:00 o'clock and trace clockwise completely around the circle. Repeat each direction several times with one palm then repeat with the other palm.

d) Arcs

(1) The Top Arc

To trace the top arc, place palm at the left end and slide the palm up, over and down to the right end, then retrace back to the starting point. Repeat several times with one palm then the other palm.

(2) The Arc Opening Right

To trace the arc opening right, place palm at the top of the curve and slide around to the bottom of the curve, then trace back to the starting point. Repeat several times with one palm then the other palm.

(3) The Arc Opening Left

To trace the arc opening left, place palm at the top of the curve and slide around to the bottom of the curve, then retrace back to the starting point. Repeat several times with one palm then the other palm.

(4) The Bottom Arc

To trace the bottom arc, place palm at the left end and slide the hand down, under and up counterclockwise to the right end, then retrace back to the starting point. Repeat several times with one palm then the other palm.

e) Diagonal Lines
   (1) Diagonal Line Starting Top Right

To trace the diagonal line to the left, place palm at the upper right end of the line and slide downward crossing the midline and continue to the lower end of the line. Retrace back to the starting point. Repeat several times with one palm then the other palm.

(2) Diagonal Line Starting Top Left

To trace the diagonal line to the right, place palm at the upper left end of the line and slide downward crossing the midline and continue to the lower end of the line. Retrace back to the starting point. Repeat several times with one palm then the other palm.

Ball Tracking Activities (2D)

Equipment Needed:
A light weight, solid colored, smooth surfaced ball approximately 8" or larger in diameter

A well-lit room or an outside area

Why ball tracking?
Ball tracking activities are associated with visual perception. As the ball comes toward the child, his eyes move inward as he tracks the ball. This inward movement of the eyes is called convergence. Convergence of the eyes is necessary for reading and for activities, such as writing, done within arm's length with the hand(s). As the ball goes away from the child, his eyes move outward as he tracks the ball. The outward movement of the eyes is called divergence.

It is important that the child learn to track a large ball first before attempting throwing and catching with a smaller ball. In each of the following tracking activities, the child tracks the ball with his eyes throughout the patterns.

The ball: Find a ball approximately 8" or larger in diameter with no seams and no texture or pebble finish. The ball should be light in weight and preferably a solid dark color. Find a well-balanced ball that bounces correctly without veering to one side or the other.

In the entire ball handling activities to follow, the adult models the same procedure as described for the child. It is recommended that the adult and the child each have a ball to use. In most of the activities, the adult will say, "Watch me. Do as I do." If only one ball is available, the adult says, "Watch me!" She demonstrates, hands the ball to the child and says; "Now you do it." The child responds.

Concept to be Learned: Exploring the Ball (2D) (Text Box 304)

1. Goal of exercise:
   • improvement in visual perception
   • improvement in convergent and divergent movements of eyes
2. What is needed:
   • 8" diameter smooth ball
3. The environment:
   • lit room with normal temperatures
   • hard, smooth floor surface
	4. Position of the child:
	   • sitting on floor with legs extended
	5. Number of repetitions:
	   • 3 hand slides around ball
	   • 3 ball hugs
	   • 3 ball rolls up and down legs
	6. How many times day/week:
	   • 3 times per week
	   • more is better, benefit never ends

The adult sits on the floor with legs extended. While leaning forward and with her eyes looking downward, she holds the ball to her chest by using the inner surfaces of her forearms, palms, and palm side of her fingers. She tells the child, "I am wrapping my arms around the ball and leaning forward to give the ball a big hug. Now you do it." The child responds by wrapping his arms around the ball while leaning forward to give the ball a big hug. The tips of his fingers should not be in contact with the ball (because the tips of the fingers are controlled by the cortical part of the brain which is not the part of the brain to be stimulated at this time.)

In this seated position with legs together and extended, the adult changes her grasp of the ball so as to hold the ball between her palms, and uses the palms of her hands to roll the ball from her chest level so that the ball can turn as it rolls from her chest, over her thighs and lower legs to her feet. She again uses the palms of her hand to return the ball to her chest in a similar fashion. The child repeats the action.

This activity is done with the palms and the palm side of the fingers in contact with the ball.

Concept to be Learned: Visually Tracking a Rolling Ball (2D) (Text Box 305)

1. Goal of exercise: • improvement in convergent and divergent movements of eyes 2. What is needed: • 8" diameter smooth solid colored ball 3. The environment: • lit room with normal temperature • hard, smooth floor surface	4. Position of the child: • sitting on floor with legs extended and spread apart 5. Number of repetitions: • 10 or more times of catching and rolling 6. How many times day/week: • 3 times per week • more is better, benefit never ends

Initially the sender and the receiver are seated close enough to each other so that their feet are touching to keep the ball from rolling away. The adult demonstrates the activity to the child, stating, "I am hugging and looking at the ball. When I roll the ball to you I will watch the ball as it rolls to you. When the ball comes to you lean forward to catch and hug the ball."

The adult first hugs the ball then uses the palms of her hands to roll the ball to the child. She visually tracks the ball as it rolls away from her toward the child. The child visually tracks the ball as it comes toward him. He leans forward to catch the ball, wraps his arms around it and brings it to his chest. The adult then says to him, "Now you roll the ball to me."

The child rolls the ball to the adult by rolling it with the palms of both hands, visually tracking the ball as it rolls away from him toward the adult.

Watch the child's eyes to be sure he is tracking the ball as it approaches him and as it rolls away from him toward the adult. As proficiency in ball handling and visual tracking develops, gradually increase the distance between sender and receiver up to twenty feet.

Concept to be Learned: Visually Tracking a Bouncing Ball (2D) (Text Box 306)

1. Goal of exercise: • improvement in convergent and divergent movements of eyes • eye-hand tracking 2. What is needed: • 8" diameter smooth solid colored ball 3. The environment: • lit room with normal temperature • hard, smooth floor surface	4. Position of the child: • sitting on floor with legs extended and spread apart or • standing and holding a ball 5. Number of repetitions: • 10 or more times of dropping, catching, bouncing, tossing a ball 6. How many times day/week: • 3 times per week • more is better, benefit never ends

Dropping and Catching the Ball

From a standing position, the adult holds the ball with both palms and inner sides of the fingers at chest height and states, "I am watching the ball," then pulls her hands apart to allow the ball to drop, and leans forward and catches it with the palms of her hands on the rebound. After demonstrating this activity the adult hands the ball to the child and says, "Now you do it, keeping your eyes on the ball." The child imitates the adult.

Dropping and catching the ball on his own is an indication that the child is developing in this ability. If he cannot drop and catch the ball from a standing position, let him sit with legs apart and drop and catch the ball from this position. If the child cannot drop and catch from the sitting position it may be necessary to return to earlier developmental exercises of Light Touch, (See page 27), Quick Tucks (See page 43), and/or Tracing Cards. (See page 81).

Return to standing position to drop and catch the ball when he is proficient at sitting and catching.

When the child is proficient with ball tracking activity, the adult demonstrates the following activity to the child. Sit with legs apart and gently bounce the ball with both hands to the child who is also sitting. The child catches and returns it with one easy bounce. The ball is caught with both hands. As control is gained in visual tracking and ball handling from the sitting position, stand and bounce the ball with both hands to the child who catches and returns it with an easy bounce. Remember to use both hands when catching and bouncing the ball, and to watch the ball as it is bounced and caught.

Palm Dribbling the Ball
When the child has a good understanding of how the ball feels in his hands and how the ball rebounds, the adult demonstrates Palm Dribbling activities to the child. She drops the ball with both hands then repetitively bounces the ball by pushing down with the palm (not the finger tips) of one hand three times, five, ten times. The child takes his turn and bounces the ball with the palm of one hand three times, five, ten, fifteen, and up to fifty times without missing a bounce. The child Palm Dribbles an equal number of times with each hand.

If the child continually "slaps" at the ball, he does not understand the feel of the ball in the palm of his hand and therefore is not ready for this activity. When you can hear the sound of the hand slapping the ball, or see the hand moving at the wrist to slap the ball, go back to exploring the ball, rolling the ball over his trunk and legs, or earlier movement patterns.

Tossing and Catching the Ball

The first step in learning to catch a tossed ball is to have adult and child stand face to face with their hands touching, palms facing upward. Working with palms facing upward prepares the child for tossing with an underhand motion. The adult starts by holding the ball against her chest, and then lowers her arms to allow the ball to roll into the child's arms. The child receives the ball and it rolls onto his arms and he traps it against his chest. The child then allows the ball to roll down his arms into the adult's arms. The adult repeats the same action and gradually moves a few feet back away from the child where an underhand tossing of the ball becomes necessary to get the ball from one to the other.

The adult then demonstrates the following tossing activity to the child: In a standing position, the adult states, "I am watching the ball," and uses both hands to toss the ball upward to a point just higher than her head, then catches it with both hands as the ball comes down. She then hands the ball to the child and tells him, "Now you do it." The adult observes the child's eyes to make sure he is tracking the ball.

Later the adult and child toss the ball underhand back and forth to each other using both hands. The adult tosses the ball so that it travels from her waist height to a point in an arc slightly above the child's head but landing at the child's chest. Each time the ball moves away from the child and each time the ball moves toward the child, he should be tracking and catching the ball and bringing it into his chest with both hands.

Eye-Hand Tracking

Equipment Needed:
Natural light or other light source coming from behind child

NOTE: The following Eye-Hand Tracking exercises are recommended for children age five and over. The adult may need to practice her demonstrations before demonstrating to the child. She needs to be sure not to move her own head as she tracks her fist.

If possible, have the child remove his glasses during tracking activities. The rims of glasses may interfere with the field of vision while performing Eye-Hand Tracking. In addition, individuals who wear glasses while Eye-Hand Tracking tend to limit their range of eye movement to the area within the limited field of vision created by the rims of their glasses. Also, wearing bifocal lenses during tracking activities may cause one to see double.

The reasons Eye-Hand Tracking exercises are so beneficial:
1. Tracking slightly above eye level helps develop comprehension and recall.
2. Tracking in the peripheral area helps develop total concepts.
3. Tracking in the lower regions directly in front of the body helps with the understanding of details.
4. Horizontal tracking helps improve ability to scan an area to locate an object and the ability to move the eyes across a line of print (reading).
5. Tracking helps in predicting location of moving objects or people as they move in space.

Comprehension and Recall Abilities

There is a relationship between looking upward and the development of comprehension and recall abilities. Anyone who has ever observed a Spelling Bee has probably noticed that when a speller is trying to recall the letters of a given word, he will often look upward. According to Ed Snapp, the reason the speller's eyes look upward is because the nervous system is scanning the brain for recall of that information. If the speller knows how to spell the word, or he thinks he knows the correct spelling, he does not have to scan and just looks straight at the judges and spells. This upward movement of the eyes is often seen in anyone trying to recall any type of information. Information gathered by Eye-Hand Tracking at eye level and above eye level is processed in the area of the brain associated with comprehension and recall.

The ability to look upward is first available during the natural birth process as the baby moves through the birth canal and views light for the first time. There are several CCDE methods involving the upward movement of the eyes to further develop and maintain the ability to comprehend and recall information.

> Watching the forward moving hand in Crawling.
> Watching the hand in Vertical Eye-Hand Tracking and the upper range of Tracking a Square Pattern.
> Looking upward when reading SNAPP Cards.
> Looking upward when doing Startle Extension.
> Tossing and catching a ball.

Eye-Hand Tracking requires one to move the arm very slowly, with the elbow and wrist straight and the hand fisted. You may need to remind the child to keep his head from moving as his eyes move to track his moving hand. When you are sitting in front of him watching him do his Eye-Tracking, you could simply touch the side of his face to let him know when he has turned his head during this exercise.

Adult instructions:
For each Eye-Hand Tracking activity described below, the adult first demonstrates the exercise to the child, and tells him, "Now you do it."

Eye-Hand Tracking exercises are done in a dimly lit room with incandescent or natural light coming from behind the child. There should be nothing in front of the child to distract his attention away from his fist. The child is sitting cross-legged with knees bent and one eye covered. The adult is sitting a few feet in front of him. The adult's role is to look for any deviations while the child performs and to help him correct any errors. Limit talking and other sensory distractions as much as possible. A silent environment with no other sensory distractions is needed. If the child's hand needs to be repositioned, gently take the child's hand and silently move his hand to the proper position or in the proper direction.

If the child is moving his fist too fast, too slow, too high, too low, pattern too small, or pattern too large, take hold of his fist and move it in the appropriate manner without comment. Release the fist and observe the pattern he is now using. If correct, let him continue; if not, re-correct and let him continue.

If the child is unable to track his fist for the entire movement, hold his fist and squeeze it until his eye locates his fist. When his eye locates the fist, move his hand from point to point (about three to four inches) in the indicated direction, holding and gently squeezing the fist. Repeat as necessary to continue the pattern. If a child is still unable to track his moving fist, have him return to the Rotation Sequence of the Arms: 1. b. (See Rotation Sequence of the Arms, page 55) where the floor supports his arm while his eyes are tracking the moving hand.

When the child is tracking a hand that is beginning to move in the peripheral area of his visual field, watch carefully to see if his eyes stop moving but the hand continue to move farther in the same direction. When the eyes stop moving but the hand continues to move, he is using a different part of his visual system and the image of the hand will not be as clear and sharp as it should be. So stop the movement of his hand at the point when the eyes have ceased to move, and begin to move his hand in the opposite direction.

If any of these deviations in Eye-Tracking are observed, the child has exceeded his background or he is fatigued. Change to another activity. (See Varied Learning Activities on page 109.) If he makes the same errors in tracking the next time this activity is done, he needs to return to earlier described tracking activities.

Concept to be Learned: Coordination of Eye-Hand Tracking (Text Box 307)

1. Goal of exercise: • develop visual perception • strengthen eye-hand coordination • enhance readiness for reading 2. What is needed: • light source coming from behind the child; eye patch optional 3. The environment: • quiet dimly lit room	4. Position of the child: • sitting crossed legged on floor • adult facing child to monitor eyes 5. Number of repetitions: • up to 10, depending on child's age and ability 6. How many times day/week: • 3 times per week • more is better, benefit never ends

Vertical Tracking Procedure

The child sits on floor with back erect, knees bent with legs crossed. The left eye is covered with the palm of the left hand cupped over the left eye so that the hand does not press on the eye (or an eye patch may be used.) The right arm is held forward, centered in front of the right eye with elbow straight, hand fisted, and trunk erect.

Vertical Tracking

The right eye tracks the right hand as the straight arm moves slowly upward and downward in a vertical line in front of the working eye. **The head does not move**, but the eye moves to maintain clear focus on the back of the fist of the extended arm.

The extended arm moves vertically upward to a position above the head only so far as the sharpness of its image does not weaken (movement of the arm stops and changes at the same time the tracking eye stops moving), then vertically downward as far as the sharpness of the image does not diminish, and is comfortable for the eye to maintain clear focus. When the eye stops at the lower and upper limits of its movement, the moving arm must also stop to allow the eye to remain focused. At these points, the arm and the eye reverse the direction of their movement.

Repeat vertical tracking with right eye covered and left eye tracking the left fist that is centered in front of the left eye.

Repeat this exercise a number of times with both eyes open, first tracking the right fist with fist centered in front of the trunk (lined up with the nose), then tracking the left fist with fist centered in front of the trunk.

In all the Eye-Hand Tracking activities, keep the moving arm straight and the head still with the eyes focused on the fist. The shoulder controls the movement of the hand through space when the arm and wrist are straight.

The developmental schedule for Eye-Hand Tracking is:
Five year olds can eventually track five times up and down. Six year olds can track six times up and down, and so on. Persons age 10 and older can work up to ten times up and down.

Horizontal Tracking Procedure

Horizontal Tracking

The child sits on floor with back erect, knees bent with legs crossed, with the left eye covered with the palm of the left hand cupped over the left eye so that the hand does not press on the eye (or an eye patch may be used.) The right arm is held forward at eye level, elbow straight, hand fisted.

The right eye follows the right hand as the straight arm moves slowly horizontally and at eye level, across the midline and back. **The head does not move**, but eye moves to maintain focus on the fist of the extended arm. When the eye stops its movement at the outer limits, the movement of the hand stops and is moved in the reverse direction.

The extended arm moves horizontally outward to a position to the side of the body but only so far as the sharpness of its image does not weaken. Then the extended arm moves horizontally inward across the midline as far as the sharpness of the image does not diminish, and is comfortable for the eye to maintain clear focus. When the eye stops at the outer and inner limits of its movement, the moving arm must also stop to allow the eye to remain focused. At these points, the arm and the eye reverse the direction of their movement.

Repeat with right eye covered and left eye tracking.

Repeat this exercise a number of times with both eyes open, first tracking the right fist, then tracking the left fist with fist centered in front of the trunk.

In all of the Eye-Hand Tracking activities, remember to keep the moving arm straight with movement coming from the shoulder and the head held still.

The developmental schedule for Eye-Hand Tracking is:
> Five year olds can eventually track five times across and back.
> Six year olds can track six times across and back, and so on. Persons age 10 and older can work up to ten times across and back.

Square Tracking Pattern

Square Tracking Pattern

The child sits on floor with back erect, knees bent and legs crossed, with the left eye covered with the palm of the left hand cupped over the left eye so that the hand does not press on the eye (or an eye patch may be used.). Start at the top, either at the upper inner corner or the upper outer corner. The right arm is held diagonally upward, elbow straight, hand fisted and at a point higher than the top of the head but only so far as keeps the sharp image of the fist in focus. Determine this starting position by having the child track his hand vertically to the point of where the eye stops moving. This is the top height for Square Tacking Pattern.

The right eye follows the right fist as the right arm moves slowly in a square pattern in front of the body. **Head does not move**. Arm extends above the head and moves to the side as far as is comfortable for the eye to maintain its ability to track and the image of the fist remains sharply in focus. The horizontal portions of the patterns are a little wider than the child's shoulder width.

Repeat with right eye covered and left eye tracking left fist.

Repeat this exercise a number of times with both eyes open, first tracking the right fist, and then tracking the left fist with fist centered in front of the trunk.

In all of the Eye-Hand Tracking activities, remember to keep the moving arm straight, and the head held still.

The developmental schedule for Eye-Hand Tracking is:
Five year olds can eventually track five times around the square
Six year olds can track six times around the square, and so on.
Persons age 10 and older can work up to ten times around the square.

The adult watches for these deviations:
Head moving
Elbow of moving arm is bent
Eye wandering from focus on fist
Fist moving to side of child or even possibly behind child
When tracking vertically the arm is not centered
When tracking horizontally the fist is not at eye level
Incorrect position of non-moving arm
Complains that his moving arm hurts
Size of the pattern changing
Slumping posture

The last three deviations are all indicators of neurological fatigue.

Recommended Sequence

Following is a recommended list for a teaching sequence of Eye-Hand Tracking.

Tracking Level One
Repeat each of these tracking patterns in five different sessions on five different days before moving to tracking Pattern Two.

1a. Vertical Tracking of fist with the eye on the same side while other eye is covered for up to 5 repetitions. Repeat with opposite eye and fist.

1b. Horizontal Tracking of fist held at eye level with the eye on the same side while other eye is covered for up to 5 repetitions. Repeat with opposite eye and fist.

1c. Horizontal Tracking with one fist held at eye level with both eyes open for up to 5 repetitions. Repeat with other fist.

When successful with Tracking Level One change to Tracking Level Two.

Tracking Level Two
NOTE: 2a and 2b are the same as 1a and 1b
Repeat each of these tracking patterns in five different sessions on five different days.

2a. Vertical Tracking of fist with the eye on the same side while other eye is covered for up to 5 repetitions. Repeat with opposite eye and fist.

2b. Horizontal Tracking of fist held at eye level with the eye on the same side while other eye is covered for up to 5 repetitions. Repeat with opposite eye and fist.

2c. Square Tracking with one eye while other eye is covered for up to 5 repetitions. Repeat with opposite eye and fist.

2d. Square tracking with one fist with both eyes open for up to 5 repetitions. Repeat with other fist.

Because of the many benefits received from Horizontal Tracking and Vertical Tracking it is preferable that both of these tracking patterns be done each day. Be sure to repeat the same pattern with each eye and each fist.

Visual Perceptions Tips

Have your child **play outside** at twilight for an extended time. This time of day provides silhouette type visual input instead of detailed images and, as a result, a more relaxed vision is used.

Discontinue the use of a night-light, if possible, so the child sleeps in absolute darkness. If the child needs to fall asleep with a dim light on, turn it off when you go to bed so his sleep is in absolute darkness. Light from outside the room (through window or from around the hall door) needs to be blocked in order for the room to be truly darkened. Keep a light handy that the child can reach if he needs to turn on a light to see to get around during the night.

It is important to limit working with fine detail, such as reading, computer work or beading. Limit or eliminate the time spent on persistent and prolonged forward vision such as viewing TV, DVDs, or video games. According to Snapp, these types of activities interfere with the developmental process, especially of younger children.

Spend more time in natural rather than artificial light.

When working at near point take a break, perhaps each 15 minutes or more, by looking away at a distance. This relaxes the eyes and helps reduce visual fatigue.

An individual should limit tasks that cause visual strain. Strain may cause fatigue, creating perceptual problems that could result in learning difficulties.

When the background and characters on that background have good contrast the impact of the visual material is much stronger; therefore, it is better retained. Dark black on white is the best contrast for most individuals.

Visual perception is best achieved when the Eye-Hand Tracking activities are done by keeping the moving arm straight and the head still with the eyes focused on the fist. Remind the child to move his eyes, not his head.

At first the child may have the ability to do only one repetition. Some children fatigue quickly in the trunk, shoulders, and arms when performing Eye-Hand Tracking and reading and may not be able to do five repetitions. Do not continue into fatigue. Fatigue is observed when the trunk becomes slumped, the movement pattern of the fisted hand changes in size or shape, or the individual complains or comments about the arm becoming tired or painful.

Be aware of the child's posture. Eye-Hand Tracking is an excellent time to assess and improve posture. The trunk will begin to slump as neurological fatigue develops. The startle extension exercise (See Startle Extension page 50) can be used to strengthen the trunk muscles and increase endurance to hold the trunk erect.

Read the Following Books:

Child's Play: Vigorous Activities With A Limited Budget, Anne Simmons and Marcella Porter, Charles C. Thomas, Springfield, Il, 1982.

The Bates Method for Better Eyesight Without Glasses, by Wm. H. Bates, M.D., Publisher: Jove Publications, Inc., New York, NY, 10016, 1978.

Health and Light, John Ott. Publisher: Devin-Adair, Greenwich, CT, 1973.

Different—The Boy Who Couldn't Write, Margie Boyd, Rockcrest Press, Georgetown, Texas, 2008.

Vision and Art: The Biology of Seeing, Margaret Livingstone, paperback, Harry N. Abram, Inc., New York, NY, 10011, 2008.

Don't assume background—Build it. Ed Snapp [3-1]

Reference

3-1. Snapp, Edward A., Jr., P.T., Quoted at Graduate Course held at TWU, 1975.

CHRONOLOGY OF READING, WRITING, AND SPELLING

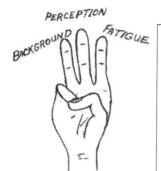

BACKGROUND: Stay within the child's developmental and educational background.

PERCEPTION: Stay within child's perceptual level for each of his senses.

FATIGUE: Stop before fatigue of the nervous system is apparent.

<u>**SNAPP Principle**</u>: **The key to successful learning is having the instructional presentation within the child's background, within the child's level of perception, and before the child becomes too fatigued for the nervous system to understand and respond correctly.**

Factors Relating to Reading and Writing

In normal language development the following chronology is seen:
1. One understands heard language before developing spoken language.
2. Spoken language is developed before one learns to read the language.
3. Ability to read the language is developed before one acquires the ability to use written language.
4. Accurate and well-expressed written form of language is the last to develop.

This sequence is followed in presenting reading, writing, and academic material to the student.

When a child is interested in a subject he learns it quickly and remembers it in greater detail. To aid a child's memory, use large objects with sharp reflective or color contrast between the background and the object that is the visual target. The **SNAPP** Cards are presented from a distance of eight feet or more, as needed for him to clearly perceive what is being presented. These distances ensure that the child is required to use far-point vision, and does not have to pull the eyes inward (converge) [4.1] to have both eyes focused on the object. These distances ensure that less visual convergence and less strong focus are required than when focusing on material held within arm's length.

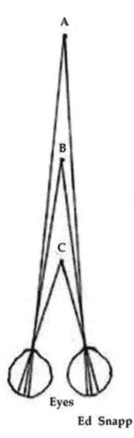

Convergence is the visual lines directed to the nearby points. When an object is brought in from a distant position (A) to a near position (B), the eyes are rotated inwardly to make the lines of vision meet at the object. The closer the object, the greater the degree of convergence (C) as indicated by the angles drawn in the illustration.

Ed Snapp

Some children may initially require the SNAPP Card to be at a distance of twenty feet or more to be able to have both eyes focused on the visual target, and to read successfully. Keep in mind that as the viewing/presenting distance increases, the size of the print and width of the stroke on SNAPP Cards, smart boards, big books, overheads, or charts must be increased in order to have each eye focusing on the desired visual target.

It is more difficult to use the eyes together to focus or fuse one's eyes on small detail within one's arm length (near point) than it is to view objects at a distance greater than the extended arm length. It is therefore important to have your developing child read **SNAPP**ed Cards, which will be presented in this chapter, at far point (eight feet or more) whenever possible so he will be more successful with reading. At true far point less stressful convergence is required. The nearer the object is to the eyes, the more the eyes move toward the bridge of the nose.

Under the age of eight, most children are not able to focus the eyes precisely on a moving target within arm's length. Normally both eyes should be focused, fused, and in motion when reading across a line of print. Insufficient convergence, or insufficient focus, or inability to fuse the eyes in motion within arm's length can be common contributors to difficulty in learning to read. "The magnitude of visual distortion is what interferes with learning." [4.2]

Good posture should always be stressed. While sitting cross-legged on the floor a child can write at arm's length on a marker board that is on the floor in front of him. This position adds greater sensation to the hip muscles, which increases postural stability.

Large muscles are developed first to provide a good foundation for smaller muscles to function correctly when performing fine motor skills. In writing, emphasis is placed on making the movements from the shoulder, as well as using the arm. Obviously the writing is done within one's arm length. Thick dark lines help to eliminate double vision that may occur when thin lines are written at this near distance. Dark wide lines are made with markers or large crayons

held within the palm. In this stage of writing **no** part of the hand is rested on the writing surface; this will enhance shoulder control. Holding the writing instrument within the palm prevents resting the hand on the writing surface.

When available, marker boards can be vertically mounted on the wall to allow the child to stand while writing large sized print (approximately 6" to 8" high). The child should write or draw at about shoulder level. It should be stressed that the child uses shoulder and arm motions while writing the larger strokes on the board, and no part of the hand rests on the writing surface.

Always watch for signs of neurological fatigue. Some examples are:
    beginning to make mistakes,
    trunk beginning to slump,
    becoming restless,
    giggling, or
    becoming unable to focus on task.

Only a short time is required to recover from neurological fatigue. But recovery **does** require stopping what one is doing and switching to a different activity that no longer stresses the same parts of the body or of the nervous system. If the current activity involves sitting, have the child change to an activity that requires standing or lying down. Changing from one activity that is done while sitting to another activity that is also done while sitting does not allow fatigue relief to the trunk of the body: the continued sitting position will continue to stress the same parts of the body.

To avoid neurological fatigue:
    keep lessons short,
    have the child change position often, and/or
    change the learning activity frequently.

Examples of Varied Learning Activities

Examples of varied learning activities are:

1) Light touch rubbing on the arms by moving arms gently across the chest (This could be done lying down, standing, or seated)
2) Sitting on the floor while responding verbally to **SNAPP** Cards
3) Crawling
4) Writing basic strokes on a marker board on the floor in response to **SNAPP** Cards while seated on the floor
5) Extension exercises
6) Eye-hand activities while seated on the floor
7) Snack break
8) Listening to a story while seated or lying down
9) Ball handling skills
10) Writing on a mounted marker board while standing
11) Flashing light activities while seated
12) Take a break, free movement or play a game

To ensure the greatest focus and attention to a task, eliminate as many distractions as is possible in the room. Distractions to a task can be the following: pictures on the wall, noisy air conditioner, background sounds and odors, hanging mobiles, bulletin boards, and other visual or auditory distractions. Charts, clocks, and all types of pictures posted around the room can be very distracting to a child. A quiet room with comfortable temperature that has plain walls, floors, and ceiling is the best learning environment.

It is best if the material being presented is emphasized while the rest of the room is de-emphasized. This can be accomplished by being in a darkened room with a projector or a spotlight focused where the teaching material will be presented, causing one's visual attention to be on the material presented. Snapp used the example of a movie theater as a controlled environment. The theater is a darkened room with a bright light projected on a large screen to maintain the viewer's attention.

In this Chapter, Chronology of Reading, Writing and Spelling, the activities start with the most basic 1D (One Dimension) activities before progressing to more complex activities of 2D (Two Dimension) and 3D (Three Dimension). Each 1D activity should be completed at a minimum of 90% accuracy before moving into any 2D activities. The same criteria apply to moving from 2D activities into 3D activities. Completion of 1D activities at the minimum of 90% accuracy provides a good foundation to building a better learner. Completion of any activity at a greater percentage of accuracy provides an even greater foundation for your child to build upon to reach his potential. For more information on **SNAPP** Dimensions refer to **SNAPP** Dimensions on page 14 and to Dimensions listed in the Glossary or Appendix A.

Language Comprehension

In normal development of language one comprehends the language he hears before acquiring spoken language or learning to read. The child originates babbling sounds such as ah, ah, ah, ga, ga, ga; ma ma ma; da da da, etc., before he is able to say words. An understanding of the heard language is inferred from a child's behavior as well as from his spoken language: example; you tell him to sit down, he sits down. He has responded to the language he has heard.

SNAPP's Sequential Developmental Levels of the Spoken Language follows.
The child:
> Echoes a single naming word or a single verb that functions as a noun for the child when he hears it. (Level 1)
> Echoes a single fact sentence or a single fact that is heard. (Level 2)
> Fills in the blank in the single fact sentence previously presented that is spoken by an adult who waits for him to say the word that goes in the blank. (Level 3)
> Does as instructed in a statement sentence spoken to him. (Level 4)

Does as instructed in a statement sentence spoken to him that includes one of the "question" words—who, when, where, what, or why. (Level 5)

Responds to a question asked of him. (Level 6)

Sometimes when a toddler is learning to talk, an adult often reads a picture book to him. The adult follows this sequence to help him develop his language. As the adult reads the story to the child the adult points to an object in the illustration such as a rabbit and names it "rabbit." The child may also touch the rabbit, but he echoes the word, "rabbit." The next time the same story is read to the child, the adult points to the rabbit and says, "This is a rabbit." The child echoes either the word "Rabbit" or the sentence spoken by the adult. At another time the same story is read and the adult points to the rabbit, and says, "This is a ___." The child supplies the missing word, "Rabbit."

A child likes to hear the same story over and over as he builds his language. At a later time when the story is again read to him, the adult says, "Show me the rabbit" and the child points to the rabbit and says, "Rabbit" or he says the sentence the adult used earlier. Most often the adult verifies the correctness of the child's response by commenting something like, "Yes, there's the rabbit!"

At still a later reading of the same story, the adult uses a statement that includes a question word, a statement that tells the child to do something, "Show me where the rabbit is," and the child points to the rabbit and talks of the rabbit, or may use the sentence the adult used: "There's the rabbit!"

At the most advanced stage, the adult reads the story to him still again, and this time asks, "Where is the rabbit?" This time the child points to or touches the rabbit and comments about the rabbit, and the adult responds with an approving comment.

Learning to read and write does involve echoing while using the **SNAPP** Word Cards or the pre-writing **SNAPP** Stroke Cards. The adult says "When you see this, say '___'," or "When you see this, make yours like mine."

Other examples of using the question words could be in a story where a boy is eating a pancake, and the adult builds up to telling him, "Show me **who** is eating the pancake." This is a statement sentence using a question word. Or in a story or picture where children are playing, one might state, "Show the girl **when** she is jumping rope." In another story a dog might be hiding under a bed in the picture, and the adult would state, "Show me **where** the dog is hiding." Perhaps another story has a goat eating a pie that is cooling on a windowsill, and later in the story the mother is puzzled about how the pie disappeared. The adult turns back to the picture of the goat eating the pie, and states, "Show me **how** the pie disappeared." The child might respond by either pointing to the appropriate picture, or act out eating the pie.

Many adults do these things intuitively. The child learns language and verbally understands it by interacting with others who already have language. The questioning word is introduced in a directive statement because no analysis is required. When the sentence starts with the questioning word, however, analysis on the child's part is required in order for him to respond correctly. Analysis is a higher "thinking order" level than that required for the child to carry out the action of a directive statement because a child would have to consider how to react instead of simply reacting.

This developmental sequence of listening comprehension is the most basic background for both expressive language and for reading comprehension. The child who has not fully developed understanding of the heard language will not freely use all parts of this sequence in his own spoken language. He is not ready for comprehending what he is reading. He needs to go back to the lowest level (echoing a single word) and proceed through all of the listening language.

As in normal language development, once basic noun concepts are learned and expressed verbally, the child begins to use phrases and then speaks in complete sentences.

Fact Teaching

Concept to be Learned: Fact Teaching, Naming Real Objects (1D) (Text Box 401)

1. Goal of exercise: • accurately name objects 2. What is needed: • objects to be named 3. The environment: • natural lighting and temperature	4. Position of the child: • walking/standing by objects 5. Number of repetitions: • as necessary for retention 6. How many times day/week: • 3 times per week • until concept is mastered

"Fact added to fact equals knowledge." (4.3)

The adult names the object; the child repeats (echoes) the word. A child must be able to know and name real objects (noun concepts) before he is taught the printed name of the object. He needs to recognize the object. He must know the object completely. When an object is named, the child should be able to point to it in the room, demonstrating that he understands the heard language. A child who is capable of speech should be able to say the name of the object demonstrating that he is able to orally express his language.

Do not allow guessing. Allowing the child to incorrectly name an object will cause confusion. If the child does not know what an object is—just tell him.

113

Concept to be Learned: Fact Sentences (2D) (Text Box 402)

1. Goal of exercise:
  • increase oral comprehension and retention of facts
2. What is needed:
  • list of simple sentences ranging from one fact to multiple facts
3. The environment:
  • natural lighting and temperature
	4. Position of the child:
	  • sitting or lying down
	5. Number of repetitions:
	  • repeat a sentence as necessary for retention of fact(s)
	6. How many times day/week:
	  • 3 times per week
	  • until concept is mastered

Single fact sentences are used first, then two fact sentences, followed by three fact sentences. Some suggested factual statements that can be used for single fact teaching are: "This is a tree." "The tree has bark." "The bark is brown." A two-fact sentence can be made from combining the two single fact sentences: "The tree has brown bark." As he becomes efficient at learning two facts, add a third fact to the sentence. He can then progress to a three-fact sentence: "The tree has rough brown bark."

This is direct teaching of factual information. Direct teaching is at the recognition level; it is concrete, efficient, and an effective way to present material. It is a simple way to learn and is easy enough for most children.

With direct teaching of the Snapp approach it is not necessary to comment on the child's performance each time. Verbalization by the adult is kept to a minimum. When an error is made, there is no comment: the material is set aside to be re-presented at a later session. If he makes the same error a second time, then set the material aside again and present it still later as if presented for the first time. If he continues to have an error for this re-presentation, he needs more experiences of the earlier developmental activities to complete this background level. Remember, when a background is complete the next concept learned is learned instantaneously unless the child is neurologically fatigued.

Reading SNAPP Silhouette Cards

Concept to be Learned: Naming Silhouettes of Known Objects (1D) (Text Box 403)

1. Goal of exercise: • see object as whole instead of parts • echo name for Silhouette on card 2. What is needed: • prepared **SNAPP** Silhouette Cards of familiar objects • spotlight 3. The environment: • quiet dim room • light focused on card **SNAPP**ed	4. Position of the child: • sitting crossed legged on floor at least 8 feet in front of card 5. Number of repetitions: • one time per card 6. How many times day/week: • 3 times per week • until concept is mastered

Once the child recognizes real concrete objects, present these known objects on large cards as solid black shapes on white cards (silhouettes). (See Appendix B for making **SNAPP** Cards.)

Use objects familiar to the child and within his vocabulary. Some examples of noun words are: "ball," "car," "tree," "box," "cup," "table." The number of syllables in the word is of little or no importance, so long as the word is within the child's verbal vocabulary. Longer noun words such as "airplane," "television," "elephant," and "computer" can be included when they are within his vocabulary. To guarantee success in reading, comprehension, and writing, the child must recognize and understand the objects before proceeding with the **SNAPP** Cards. We acknowledge that some objects, for example, prehistoric creatures and dinosaurs, are not actually in the child's own environment but prehistoric animals may be in his present level of interest. He recognizes and understands these objects when he listens to stories, sees their pictures, or reads about them.

The child must be able to recognize the difference between light and dark areas in order to read the Silhouette Cards—that is why use of the flashing light may be necessary for a child who cannot read silhouettes. It is not necessary to use a great number of Silhouette Cards; but use enough of them to help the child realize that the silhouette stands for the object. Usually fifteen to twenty Silhouette Cards may be sufficient. Since a younger child enjoys using silhouettes, many more Silhouette Cards may be used. When a new subject is presented to your child, use Silhouette Cards to introduce objects of that subject and use **SNAPP** Cards to introduce the new subject's vocabulary.

In this exercise as well as other exercises in this book, the suggested sitting position of the child is with legs crossed. However, if your child cannot sit cross-legged or needs to change his position, he may sit in a chair or on the floor in a position more comfortable to him.

The child sits with legs crossed on the floor at a distance of at least eight feet in front of the adult who will **SNAPP** the card. Sitting on the floor is a less complex skill than is sitting in a chair. Also, the floor provides more muscle input, which helps to calm the hyperactivity of a younger child. If you are working with several children, have them sit in front of the adult so each child has a clear vision of the **SNAPP** Card. However, do not allow a child to sit at an angle of more than 15 degrees from the center of the card because the greater angle distorts the print.

If necessary for maintaining the child's attention on the card, this activity can be done in a quiet dark room with a spotlight or lamp shining on the card. As the card is **SNAPP**ed it is rotated toward the child so the child can read the silhouette on the card.

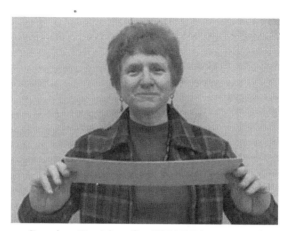

Starting Position for **SNAPP**ing a Card

Grip the card at the midpoint of the sides with your thumb and index finger of both hands Keep the card with the silhouette rotated slightly toward you, (it will be upside down as you view it) not visible to the child (See picture above showing the Starting Position for **SNAPP**ing a Card.) The card is held at a level above the child so that the child can easily see the silhouette when the card is SNAPPed. The adult may stand or sit as long as the child is looking upward at the card from a distance of at least eight feet away from the **SNAPP**ed card. By looking upward at the card, the child will be using that part of the brain that is associated with comprehension. By having the child sit at least eight feet away from the **SNAPP**ed card, the child's eyes are looking straight ahead and he is using that part of the brain associated with recognition.

SNAPP the card quickly! Snapp suggested that the speed of rotation be a hundredth of a second (and only he could rotate a card that fast!). At this speed the child will see the silhouette as a <u>whole </u>instead of as a silhouette of detailed parts. This rotation at a rapid speed creates an optical illusion where the object on the card—whether the object is a silhouette, basic stroke, or a word—will appear in its entirety as if the card is momentarily suspended in space. This optical illusion effect is called the Thaumatrope Illusion. The child who reads the rapidly rotated card is working on that part of the brain associated with recognition, comprehension, and dominance.

Make sure when **SNAPP**ing the card that it remains stationary in space by keeping the forearms steady during the entire rotation. It is recommended that the adult stand in front of a mirror and practice **SNAPP**ing the card many times to be sure that the rotating card is steady in space before using this technique in a learning situation.

Tell the child what each Silhouette Card is going to be before **SNAPP**ing the card. For example, the adult, in a strong, confident voice, says, "When you see this, say 'ball'!" Then the card is **SNAPP**ed. The child echoes, in a strong, confident voice "Ball!" The child should name the silhouette with confidence. If his voice sounds unsure or questioning, present the card again, giving the instruction in an especially strong voice for the word being presented.

When the child responds in a strong voice the adult **SNAPP**s the same card a second time but provides no verbal cue. When the child responds correctly place the card in a stack. These cards are to be **SNAPP**ed later without a verbal cue. If the child makes an error on the second trial, it may be the result of neurological fatigue or of his visual perception background.

These **SNAPP** Silhouette Cards are read

"Ball"   "Cup"

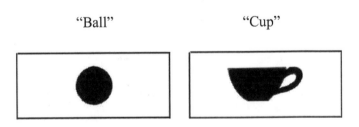

If the child hesitates or misidentifies the image re-teach it, saying the name of the image, and **SNAPP**ing the card again. If he says he cannot identify the silhouette or hesitates in naming it—tell him the word. He will needs more of the Activity: Contrasting Dark and Light described on page 75.

Require quick, instantaneous responses from the child. This will allow him to recall it automatically when he sees it in the future. Have him speak loudly and clearly to make sure he is saying the word correctly. Require accuracy! You are building background!

Using silhouettes makes the transition from concrete objects to representative "words" a less abstract process.

Concept to be Learned: Identifying Seven Basic Colors (1D) (Text Box 404)

1. Goal of exercise:
  • discriminating among colors
  • associating name with color
2. What is needed:
  • prepared **SNAPP** Color Cards
  • spotlight
3. The environment:
  • quiet dim room
  • light focused on card **SNAPP**ed
	4. Position of the child:
	  • sitting crossed legged on floor at least 8 feet in front of card
	5. Number of repetitions:
	  • one time per card
	6. How many times day/week:
	  • 3 times per week
	  • until concept is mastered

The basic colors of red, yellow, orange, blue, green, purple, and black are also introduced on **SNAPP** Cards and presented in this order. Each Color Card is completely covered by a single color. A child does not interpret "white" as a color; so do **not** introduce white at this time. **Do not use colored shapes to teach a color** as the child may be associating the shape with the naming word rather than the color. Teach the Color Card first; teach the printed word later.

If a child needs to remain working in this stage for a longer time, other hues or shades may be introduced as **SNAPP** Color Cards, but each must have its own distinctive name, and each such name must be applied correctly and consistently.

Reading Sequence

The following is the developmental sequence that Snapp suggests for presenting reading on **SNAPP** Word Cards:

1. Nouns: "ball," "car," "tree," "box"
2. Size adjectives with noun: "big ball," "small ball"
3. Color adjectives with noun: "red ball," "blue box"
4. Indicator words: "a," "an," "the," with a noun: "a box," "an apple"
5. Three word phrases and prepositional phrases: "a big ball," "in the box"
6. Separate cards for each form of the verb to be: "is," "was," "am," "were," "are"
7. Simple sentences using previously learned words: "the ball is red"
8. Verbs that have noun concepts: "run," "sleep," "jump"
9. Syllable phonics: (au to mo bile)

Please notice that only lower case letters are being used at this tine,

1. Reading Noun Words (1D)

   Concept to be Learned: Reading Noun Words (Text Box 405)

1. Goal of exercise: • recognize the word • read the word aloud 2. What is needed: • prepared **SNAPP** noun word cards • spotlight 3. The environment: • quiet dim room • light focused on card **SNAPP**ed	4. Position of the child: • sitting crossed legged on floor at least 8 feet in front of card 5. Number of repetitions: • one time per card per session 6. How many times day/week: • 3 times per week • until concept is mastered

When the child has been successful at reading silhouettes, words may be introduced. Work with the silhouette nouns first. Examples: "ball," "car," "tree," "box," "cup," "table." The number of syllables in the word is of little or no importance. Longer noun words, such as airplane, television, elephant, computer can be included if they are within the child's vocabulary and interest. Use **SNAPP** Cards to present words after the object that the word represents can be recognized by the child. It might be necessary to stay with silhouettes for an additional time period for some children.

The cards should be at least 4" high and 11" wide. Material for the **SNAPP** Cards can be made from poster board or card stock. (See Appendix B) Some teachers use copy paper (regular or legal size folded in half lengthwise) that they hold on a stiff backing completely covered by the same type white paper. The **SNAPP** Cards should have letter **strokes** (strokes are used to form a printed letter) that are one-quarter inch to one-half inch wide. This width works for most children. But if the child is still having problems seeing the strokes, make the strokes wider and the letters larger. Doing so will likely require the use of a larger rectangular card.

If the word is too long or too large for the size paper being used, create a larger sized card that allows margins on each side. The margins are needed for grasping the card without your fingertips or thumb covering any part of the black image or letters.

You are now ready to **SNAPP** the first word card. The first word (be sure your child recognizes these objects) should be "ball." The others follow in this order: "car," "tree," "box," "cup," and "table." This order is recommended because each word has a unique outline shape that is different from all the other outlines of words in the set. Initially words that rhyme are not presented at the same time.

The adult must be aware of the differences in outline shapes in selecting words to be presented to the child. Word outline shapes as such, however, are never presented to the child.

Following are examples of word outline shapes:

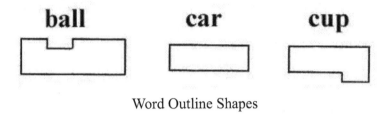

Word Outline Shapes

Each of the silhouettes that has been presented has a name represented by a written word. The name identifies it. For example, the ball silhouette has the written name "ball."

When introducing the printed word names to the child, the adult makes sure that her verbalization of reading the **SNAPP** Card aloud contains the qualities she will expect in the child's verbal response. These qualities are a quick response with a rapid, clear, and loud voice. The adult says, "When you see the word ball, say 'Ball'," then **SNAPP**s the card.

This card is read

"ball"

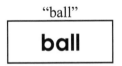

The child quickly responds in a clear, loud voice, "Ball."

DO NOT allow discussion at this time! DO NOT ask him for letter sounds or what is the first letter of the word! DO NOT let him guess! Repeat the **SNAPP** several times to verify that the child reads the word correctly and instantly.

If he is having difficulty reading the word, he is not ready for using **SNAPP** Word Cards. Stay within his perceptual level of development by continuing with flashing lights and silhouette cards at this time.

Never have the silhouette and the word on the same card.

If he read that card without difficulty present another **SNAPP** Card that has a different outline shape and starts with a different letter, like **car,** so that the child can easily perceive the uniqueness of the word. You say, "**Car**" and **SNAPP** the card; the child says, "**Car.**" For a young child, mix up the two words and present them without saying the words again to see if he correctly reads each word with an instantaneous response.

Give another word with a different yet distinctive outline shape. For example, **tree**. You say, "**Tree**" and **SNAPP** the card; the child says "**Tree.**" Repeat the **SNAPP** several times without saying the word again to verify that the child reads it correctly and instantly.

Review all words presented so far (ball, car, tree, box, cup, and table). Re-order the **SNAPP** Cards to provide a varied order of presentation. If a mistake is made, set that card aside and reintroduce (re-teach) the word at a later time. Do not emphasize the error; change to another activity. (See Examples of Varied Learning Activities on page 109 of this chapter.)

Watch for wandering eyes, wiggly bodies, or mistakes. These indicate that the child is neurologically fatigued and he needs the activity changed.

After these words are known, add more noun words. When the child can read 20 or more words correctly, introduce three more words that start with the same letter but have distinctive outline shapes. Example, **boy, bat, book or turtle, truck, trains**. At this time the child is reading the total word and understanding its configuration. Be sure to include multi-syllable words that are familiar to the child. Examples: butterfly, elephant, computer, etc.

Reinforcement and review are necessary; the more review, the better. Review new words three to four times a day. Review old words three to four times per week.

Do not use capital letters when introducing words. Use only lower case letters. **Capitals** are presented later when the child is already reading sentences that are initially presented without the first word capitalized. In this way the child has only one capital letter to learn at a time. Capital letters, however, can be used on proper nouns, such as a child's name, but do not point out the difference when presenting proper nouns. **Never use words printed with all capital letters on SNAPP Word Cards.**

Initially it is best to present five words or fewer per day. Three words that are vividly distinctive in shape and concept may be presented in a single session. Examples: car, box, tree; or cup, ball, table. For many children one or two words a day may be enough. The number of words is unique to the individual, depending on the child's stage of development. Later, of course, as the child's background, perception, and fatigue levels develop, the number of words presented daily may be increased.

2. Reading Adjectives with Nouns (2D)

    Concept to be Learned: Reading Nouns with Adjectives (Text Box 406)

1. Goal of exercise:
 • recognize and read
  aloud two word phrases
2. What is needed:
 • prepared **SNAPP**
  adjective-plus-noun
  word cards
3. The environment:
 • quiet dim room
 • light focused on card
  SNAPPed
	4. Position of the child:
	 • sitting crossed legged
	  on floor at least 8 feet in
	  front of card
	5. Number of repetitions:
	 • one time per card
	6. How many times day/week:
	 • 3 times per week
	 • until concept is
	  mastered

After the child possesses 30 to 50 noun words, introduce size adjectives such as "big," "little," "large," or "small," **with a noun**. The new instruction for the child is: "You just read 'box,' you can read 'big box'." When you see this, say, "big box'."

These cards are read

If a child is not able to handle two-word phrases, continue to teach him single nouns while working within his developmental background, perception, and fatigue levels.

3. Reading Color Adjectives (2D)

Next introduce color adjective words, using only the basic colors: red, yellow, orange, blue, green, purple, and black. The new instruction is: "You just read 'box.' If you can read 'box', you can read 'red box'. When you see this, say, 'Red box'."

This card is read

4. Reading Indicator Words in Phrases (2D)

Introduce indicator words (adjectives) such as "a," "an," and "the" with words they can already read. Examples of phrases are: "a ball," "an apple," "the ball," "a car," "the apple," etc. The new instruction is: "You just read 'ball.' If you can read 'ball,' you can read 'a ball.' When you see this, say 'A ball'," **SNAPP** the card. The child says, "A ball."

These cards are read

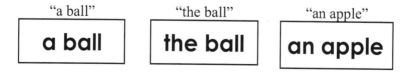

5. Three Word Phrases (2D)

Concept to be Learned: Reading Three Word Phrase Containing a Noun (Text Box 407)

1. Goal of exercise: • recognize and read aloud three word phrases 2. What is needed: • prepared **SNAPP** three word phrase cards • spotlight 3. The environment: • quiet dim room • light focused on card **SNAPP**ed	4. Position of the child: • sitting crossed legged on floor at least 8 feet in front of card 5. Number of repetitions: • one time per card 6. How many times day/week: • 3 times per week • until concept is mastered

The first three word phrases use words already learned by the child. The phrase consists of an indicator word, a size or color adjective, and a noun. The phrase cards, like all other **SNAPP** Cards, are **SNAPP**ed at a tenth of a second or less. All **SNAPP** Cards for three word phrases are of the same size. The new instruction is: "You just read 'red box'. If you can read 'red box', you can read 'the red box'. When you see this, say 'The red box'."

These cards are read

"the red box"

the red box

"the big ball"

the big ball

Before three-word prepositional phrases are introduced, give the child an opportunity to experience the concepts. A preposition is always used to indicate the relationship of one object to another.

The child must understand the complete concept of prepositions, such as "in," "on," "beside," "with," "under," etc., before presenting the word to be read in a phrase.

These concepts can be taught concretely by having the child move through these positions relative to another object. Or have him manipulate an object, such as a toy car in relationship to another object such as a desk. He can place the car "in a desk," "on a desk," "beside a desk," "under a desk," and other places using prepositional phrases.

These cards are read

"on the desk"   "under the desk"

| **on the desk** | **under the desk** |

Time relationships can also be used in prepositional phrases. Examples are: "after Monday," "during lunch," "before the game," "between 7 and 8 o'clock."

6. Reading Various Forms of To Be (2D)

Concept to be Learned: Reading Forms of "to be" (Text Box 408)

1. Goal of exercise: • recognize single word forms of the verb "to be" 2. What is needed: • prepared **SNAPP** "to be" single word cards • spotlight 3. The environment: • quiet dim room • light focused on card **SNAPP**ed	4. Position of the child: • sitting crossed legged on floor at least 8 feet in front of card 5. Number of repetitions: • one time per card 6. How many times day/week: • 3 times per week • until concept is mastered

A separate card for each form of "to be": (is), (was), (were), (am), (are) needs to be created. Early in the teaching of reading, when the child has a number of nouns and descriptive words, "is" is the only verb on a card by itself. Using the verb "is" paves the way for putting short phrases together to form sentences. Later the other forms of "to be" are taught separately so they can be used to create simple sentences.

When presenting the first form of "to be," the adult says, "When you see this say 'Is'," and **SNAPP**s the card; the child says, "Is." Repeat as needed. After this verb can be read the child is ready to read simple sentences.

For example, "The ball is red." "The cup is on the table." "The car is in the box." Later, as more nouns and phrases are mastered other forms of "to be" can be used.

7. Simple Sentences (2D)

   Concept to be Learned: Reading Simple Sentences (Text Box 409)

1. Goal of exercise: • read sentences from word cards placed on floor	4. Position of the child: • standing over **SNAPP** Cards that are face down on floor
2. What is needed: • one-word **SNAPP** Cards up to four-word **SNAPP** Cards.	5. Number of repetitions: • repeatedly with various **SNAPP** word card sentences
3. The environment: • well lit quiet room	6. How many times day/week: • 3 times per week • until concept is mastered

After the child learns phrases and the verb "is", the cards can be combined to make a simple sentence. The **SNAPP** Cards are used in the following manner:

SNAPP the first Phrase Card. For example, "the ball."
*Note there are not any capital letters on this card.
The child reads it.
The adult places the card face down on the floor slightly to the left of the child's center.

SNAPP the "is" verb card.
The child reads it.
The adult places the card face down on the floor centered in front of the child and in line with the first card.

SNAPP the ending Phrase Card. For example, "in the box."
The child reads it.
The adult places the Phrase Card face down on the floor slightly to the right of the child's center and in line with the other Cards.

The child turns over the first Card, stands and looks down at the Card and reads it. The child continues to turn and read each Card. Then he reads all the Cards as a complete sentence. Standing is used because it maintains a viewing distance greater than arm's length, allowing distance for far point convergence and focus.

When the Cards are read aloud as they are turned over the cadence and phrasing is that of speaking a sentence; it prevents the separated "word calling" reading often used by poor readers. This helps build reading fluency.

The child then re-reads the entire sentence, using the same cadence and phrasing as is used for speaking a sentence.

For example, "the ball is in the box"

the ball	**is**	**in the box**

This procedure is used repeatedly with different Phrase Cards.

Notice that the phrasing is the same as that in our speech inflection pattern, as is used by fluent readers. We emphasize that this also prevents the "single word calling" used by non-fluent readers.

After the child has acquired many nouns in his vocabulary and can use simple phrases and sentences, progress to **SNAPP**ing a four-word phrase or a four-word sentence. Use two words on each of two lines on a large **SNAPP Card**. Later, progress to three words on each of the two lines. These cards may contain a meaningful phrase or a complete sentence.

Notice that there are still no capital letters on any of these cards. This allows the words on the cards to be used anywhere in the sentence. Later the child will be told that sentences begin with capital letters.

the ball is red	**the ball is on the table**

8. Verbs With Noun Concept (1D)

After the child understands nouns and the verb "is", other verbs are introduced that have noun concepts. The child must understand the verb that is being taught. A verb has a noun concept if it describes an activity or can be acted out; for example, "jump!" "roll!" "skip!" "sit!" etc. He should also be able to use each verb in a spoken sentence. Only then should a verb be presented on a **SNAPP Card** as a separate word. For example, the adult could **SNAPP** the word "jump" and the child could respond by saying "Jump" and then he jumps.

There is a proper **SNAPP** time and **SNAPP** sequence for transitioning from reading from a **SNAPP** Card to reading small print from a book. The sequence is as follows:

1. Objects in a short book are named.
2. The vocabulary from a short book is learned using the **SNAPP** Cards.
3. The phrases and verbs are taught using **SNAPP** Phrase Cards.
4. The Phrase and Verb Cards are read from the floor.
5. The entire sentence is read from turning over the Cards on the floor.
6. The same sentence is presented in large print in single page or book format for the child to read at his straightened arm's distance.
7. Using the same material as used in #5, the sentence is read from the book while seated at a proper fitting desk or table.

Name the objects mentioned in a short book. Teach the vocabulary of a short book that uses simple sentences; proceed through the **SNAPP** Phrase and Verb Cards, etc, and end by letting the child read the entire book by himself. You may need to create the book in order to use his reading vocabulary. All new vocabulary words are to be taught using **SNAPP** Cards.

Keep the book within his perception range by having it in large bold print and insist it be held at extended arm's distance. Stories can also be written on a flip chart using large black print made using wide strokes, and read from an eight-foot distance. The child can lic on his stomach on the floor at straightened arm's length from the book, with the book propped up against the baseboard. The child can turn the pages for himself. This positioning ensures that the book is at a distance that causes the least amount of stress to the visual system.

The adult can create a book using the child's reading vocabulary. The book can be printed on a computer. Use landscape style on copy paper. Arrange the printing so that you will have only one short sentence at the bottom of each page. This leaves him room to draw a picture on the top half of the page that represents the content of the sentence. Create a title page and stack the pages in proper order. Staple the pages together.

9. Syllable Phonics (3D)

Concept to be Learned: Syllable Phonics (Text Box 410)

1. Goal of exercise:
  • read syllable phonics
2. What is needed:
  • syllable **SNAPP** Cards
  • spotlight
3. The environment:
  • quiet dark room
  • light focused on card
    SNAPPed
	4. Position of the child:
	  • on the floor, cross
	    legged, at least 8' from
	    front of card
	5. Number of repetitions:
	  • one time per card
	6. How many times day/week:
	  • 3 times per week
	  • until concept is
	    mastered

Introduce syllable phonics <u>only after the child is reading and spelling well</u>. Snapp completely disapproved teaching letter-sound phonics when a child is first learning to read. Analysis may stop the developmental process by causing the child to see just individual letters. Snapp considered the letter-sound phonics approach to be too analytical for the child's developmental level.

Snapp had the insight to use "syllable phonics", but to save the teaching of syllable phonics until after the child is aware of reading and spelling patterns. A word is made up of one or more syllables. Each syllable contains one vowel sound. Where the word is divided creates the syllable spelling that controls the vowel sound. Spelling patterns and sometimes the syllable divisions can also affect the sound of a consonant or consonant group within a word.

When syllable phonics is taught, split words that the child already knows into syllables. Precise enunciation of the syllables within a word helps with speaking, reading, and spelling. When printing the **SNAPP** Card, use a blank letter space between syllables and pronounce the word in syllables. **Be sure that each word is**

correctly separated into syllables. Correct spelling and division of words can be checked in American dictionaries.

com pu ter

el e phant

NOTE: No hyphens are used to separate the syllables—only one empty space is used to separate syllables on the **SNAPP** Syllable Card.

For all information presented, work for 90% accuracy or better. If the child's developmental background is developed up to the level of information being presented he will be able to achieve that level of accuracy, and to understand the material being presented.

Handwriting Sequence

Snapp's activities often serve as the background for many different functions. For example, Pounding and Rubbing found in the Foundation of Movement Chapter (page 33) build basic sensations and also build the background for Handwriting. The following is the developmental sequence that Snapp suggests for presenting handwriting:

1. Open Palm Tracing For Pre-writing (horizontal line, vertical line, circle, etc., see page 134) with movement from the shoulder.
2. Basic Strokes (See Appendix B) from **SNAPP**ed Cards (using large writing instrument held within palm) with movement from the shoulder as well as using movement of the elbow. The **hand does not rest** on the paper or writing surface.

Before well-coordinated writing can take place the child should have control of the large core muscles of the back as well as the muscles of the hips, shoulders, arms, and hands. Without good posture, controlled handwriting is almost impossible because the child will be constantly shifting his body. The child's nervous system must sense the positions of all body parts in order to manage the body's stability. Light touch stimulation of the side of the fingers aids in enhancing handwriting.

Large writing activities become part of the child's sensory motor control. His writing eventually requires less conscious effort as it becomes more automatic. Using large writing techniques produces better handwriting as movement and control of the shoulder, elbow, wrist, and fingers becomes more integrated.

SNAPP's Deep Pressure (See page 36) helps the child understand body awareness. This understanding improves how his muscles work.

Deep pressure sensations control the amount of contact force used by the hand when writing. Incomplete understanding of sensations often result in the child having handwriting problems such as "white knuckles", broken pencils, holes torn in paper, dropped pencils, or very light marks on the paper.

Your child may need to participate in the **SNAPP** developmental activities in the Foundation of Movement Chapter to gain adequate control of his body's movements and sensations.

By participating in these activities, even a well-integrated child will enhance his sensory motor control and visual memory.

Open Palm Tracing For Pre-writing (2D)

Concept to be Learned: Open Palm Tracing for Hand Writing (Text Box 411)

1. Goal of exercise:
  • use of shoulder/back muscles appropriate for this activity
2. What is needed:
  • large tracing cards
3. The environment:
  • well lit room
4. Position of the child:
  • on the floor, cross legged, trunk erect, leaning forward so palm of hand can reach line being traced
	• cards are placed in front of child
	5. Number of repetitions:
	  • several times a day with different **SNAPP** Tracing Cards
	6. How many times day/week:
	  • 3 times per week
	  • until concept is mastered

Some children tend to draw very small images and write very small. By doing this, the small muscles of the hand are stimulated and the use of appropriate posture and shoulder muscles is avoided. These small images are also more stressful on vision than the larger images. In order to boost a child's complete development, use flat palm and forearm sliding. While sitting at a table with a smooth, wet surface, the child slides the palm of one hand across the surface several times. Repeat with the other hand.

Then with the inner forearm (elbow to palm) in contact with the surface, the child moves the forearm in various patterns. The trunk remains stationary with movement coming from the shoulder. Repeat with the other hand and forearm.

The movements using the entire arm from shoulder to palm are the developmental foundation for handwriting and drawing.

Some suggestions for wetting the flat surface:
 water
 lotion
 shaving cream
 chocolate pudding

Another way to add to your child's development is to use a wide line for the child to trace that naturally makes the movements large. Large strokes involve movement in the shoulder and stimulate the back muscles. Using large movements that require use of large muscles is appropriate to his current developmental level.

These large shoulder movements are important because they allow automatic learning of the total concept. Small, fine motor activities require mostly visual and small muscle control and do not develop the automatic nervous system. **Small, fine motor activities are the end result—not a beginning developmental procedure.**

Each large Tracing Card contains a basic design that is one of nine basic strokes used to form printed letters. Large Tracing Cards are not **SNAPP**ed, but are placed on the floor in front of the child, who traces the design with his flat palm. All basic strokes for handwriting are traced in only one direction, from left to right. Tracing with the palm is first done by one hand and then with the palm of the other hand. **It is best for the adult to be beside the child to demonstrate this activity in order for the child to be aware of the correct directionality of the strokes.**

See page 80 to review the directions for Open Palm Tracing for Visual Development. **Open Palm Tracing for Pre-writing differs in two ways from Open Palm Tracing for Visual Development.**

1) The child traces the designs only in the handwriting direction, and
2) he lifts his hand at the end of each stroke to return it to the starting position.

Basic Strokes From **SNAPP**ed Cards (2D)

Snapp never found a commercial product to satisfy him as an implement to prepare for handwriting. The following are his directions for using the instrument he designed for this purpose. (See Appendix D)

Equipment needed: writing implement, writing fluid and container, large writing surface (or a blank rectangular paper), towel or paper towels, and **SNAPP** Cards.

It may be necessary to emphasize the act of lifting the hand holding the writing implement at the end of tracing in the single direction in order for the child to clearly perceive that this Writing Basic Strokes is different from the earlier tracing activities.

Concept to be Learned: Writing Basic Strokes from **SNAPP**ed Cards (Text Box 412)

1. Goal of exercise:
  • write the one, two, or three **SNAPP** Stroke Cards
2. What is needed:
  • large writing surface
  • writing implement
  • container of writing fluid
  • **SNAPP** Stroke Cards with one, two, or three strokes
  • towel or paper towel
3. The environment:
  • well lit quiet room
	4. Position of the child:
	  • seated on the floor, cross legged
	  • trunk erect
	  • leaning forward so hand with implement can reach writing surface in front of him
	5. Number of repetitions:
	  • 2 to 3 times a day
	6. How many times day/week:
	  • 3 times per week
	  • until concept is mastered

The rubber ball handle of the handwriting instrument (or a sponge) is placed in the palm of the child's preferred hand for making the pre-writing strokes. This ball eliminates the use of the fingertips and stimulates large shoulder movements. Using the entire palm to hold the instrument builds automatic and coordinated large motor functions and connects the arm movements with the shoulder.

With the use of dark tempera paint, the sponge (the writing tip of the implement) makes an impressive large, dark line on butcher paper, white board or any other acceptable large area. Large markers and large chalk are less desirable, but will work when held within the palm of the hand.

The basic strokes for writing are introduced with **SNAPP Cards** that have only one stroke on each card. The cards in the first group of basic strokes are introduced in the following order:
  a. Vertical Line;
  b. Horizontal Line,
  c. Circle.

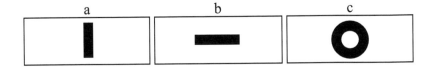

The child writes vertical lines from top to bottom and horizontal lines from left to right. Circles are written in clockwise (starting at 10 o'clock) and counterclockwise (starting at 2 o'clock) directions since both are used in writing. All one-symbol **SNAPP** Cards should be the same size so they can be handled easily.

The child sits cross-legged on the floor with a large marker board (12" by 18" or 18" by 24") in front of him. The adult says, "Make yours like mine," then **SNAPP**s the card. The child writes what he sees as the stroke card is **SNAPP**ed.

Position for Pre-writing

138

After the vertical, horizontal, and circle strokes are mastered, half circles are introduced in this order:

a. Top Curve;
b. Curve Opening Right;
c. Curve Opening Left;
d. Bottom Curve.

Make sure that these are complete **half circles** because some children perceive shallow curves as straight lines.

Diagonal lines can now be added.

a. Diagonal Line Starting Top Right

b. Diagonal Line Starting Top Left

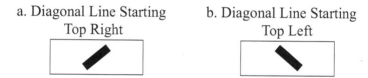

After the child consistently demonstrates 90% accuracy in replicating each of these single stroke cards, cards with two symbols are then introduced. Use the same instructional phrase, "Make yours like mine" and pointing to the child's left side add, "Start on this side." Then **SNAPP** the card!

When these cards are rotated 180 degrees a new sequence is created. For example, the horizontal-vertical card becomes vertical-horizontal when rotated 180 degrees. The horizontal-circle card becomes a circle-horizontal card when rotated 180 degrees, and the circle-vertical becomes a vertical-circle when rotated 180 degrees.

Do not repeat the same symbol side by side on the same card. If you do, the child might perceive that he is seeing double.

Once mastered, the curves can also be added to the other basic strokes to make more two-symbol cards.

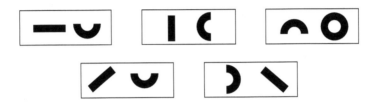

When two-symbol cards are mastered with 90% accuracy, three symbol cards can be introduced. Make all three-symbol cards the same length and height so that they can be handled easily, holding three to five cards at a time. As each number of symbols on a card is mastered, increase the number of symbols to four, five, then to seven symbols on a card. Mastery of writing five to seven symbols on a card aids in visual memory and is the developmental foundation for written spelling.

When using two and three-stroke **SNAPP** Cards, expect the child to follow the writing sequence from left to right. In doing so, you are teaching good orientation to reading and writing. You say, "Start on the left side" as you point to his left and "Go to the right" as you point to his right.

If a child cannot do an activity with 90% accuracy, he may be neurologically fatigued or his background is not complete. It is necessary to change activities or return to a previous developmental level and reinforce the developmental exercises.

In writing, letters are perceived as sitting on a base line. Some letters are tall, some letters are short, and some letters are a combination of tall and short. Some letters extend below the base line (tailed letters) and some letters are a combination of short and tailed. To aid in the development of different space relations, some basic strokes are placed above an imaginary base line, others on the base line, and still others below the base line—as is seen in the **SNAPP** pre-writing cards above. This relative spacing of the strokes on the card is part of the accuracy in the child's response.

Spelling

1. Writing Basic Strokes for Spelling (2D)

    The use of three symbol pre-writing cards and the written response are considered to be pre-spelling cards. The child is learning to perceive parts of a letter or letters, and is responding to the presentation in written form.

Concept to be Learned: Duplicating Writing Patterns of Basic Strokes (Text Box 413)

1. Goal of exercise: • replicate with 100% accuracy three to five pre-writing strokes on **SNAPPed** cards 2. What is needed: • large writing surface, implement and container of writing fluid • **SNAPP** Stroke Cards with three to five strokes 3. The environment: • well lit quiet room	4. Position of the child: • sitting on the floor, cross legged • trunk erect • leaning forward so palm of hand can reach line being traced • cards are placed in front of child 5. Number of repetitions: • 2-3 repetitions 6. How many times day/week: • 3 times per week • until concept is mastered

The child sits cross-legged on the floor with a large marker board (12" by 18" or 18" by 24") in front of him. The adult says, "Make yours like mine," then **SNAPP**s the card. The child writes what he sees as the Stroke Card is **SNAPP**ed.

A child needs to have the ability to respond accurately to **SNAPP**ed pre-writing cards having three to five pre-writing symbols before attempting written spelling.

1. Oral Spelling (2D)

   Now is the time to teach the letter names from **SNAPP** Cards. *The name of each letter is not taught in isolation but within the context of spelling the word aloud.*

   Concept to be Learned: Naming Letters that Form Words (Text Box 414)

1. Goal of exercise:
  • 100% accuracy reading and spelling aloud
2. What is needed:
  • one syllable **SNAPP** Cards having three to five letters progressing to long words
  • spotlight
3. The environment:
  • quiet dark room
  • spotlight focused on card as it is **SNAPP**ed
	4. Position of the child:
	  • standing or seated on the floor cross legged
	  • at least eight feet in front of **SNAPP**ed card
	5. Number of repetitions:
	  • one time per card
	  • repeat **SNAPP** without cue
	6. How many times day/week:
	  • 3 times per week
	  • until concept is mastered

   Ability to recite the alphabet is not necessary for learning to read or to write spelling. **Names of letters are not taught in isolation.** Eventually learning the alphabetical order of the letters can be taught for use in oral spelling, filing, or looking up words or names in a telephone book, dictionary or encyclopedia.

One-syllable words composed of three-to-five-letters, that are part of the child's reading vocabulary, are used first. The child needs to know the object that the word represents. He needs to be able to read a word before learning to spell that word because knowing what the word looks like will help in knowing how to put the word together. The child does oral spelling with a strong confident voice.

The pattern used for presentation is as follows:

1. **SNAPP** the word card.
2. Read the word.
3. Name the letters.
4. State the word that was spelled orally.

Example:
The adult says, "When you read this word, say 'Ball, b a l l, ball'." Remember to use a strong firm voice to state what the child is to actually say in response to reading the word and telling how to spell it. **Clearly separate the names of the letters; this is part of the modeling you do for the child.**

SNAPP the card, the child echoes loudly, "Ball, b   a   l   l, ball."

Continue by presenting words from the child's reading vocabulary for the child to spell orally.

The child progresses to written spelling only after he has mastered the oral spelling of a large number of words. Written Spelling is initiated before presentation of Syllable Phonics.

As a result of his involvement in CCDE exercises, a child will progress and excel in spelling as he:
   1) improves his visual memory by working with basic symbols,

2) improves his comprehension and recall abilities (see Comprehension and Recall Abilities on page 92) by looking upward as he reads various **SNAPP**ed cards,
3) improves his comprehension and recall abilities by eye-hand tracking in the upper vertical range, and
4) acquires the concept of letters and letter sounds by reading, spelling, and saying what he just read and spelled from the **SNAPP** word cards.

4. Written Spelling (2D)

    Concept to be Learned: Orally Spelling and Writing Words (Text Box 415)

1. Goal of exercise:
  • 100% accuracy
    in writing words
    SNAPPed on cards
2. What is needed:
  • large writing surface,
    implement and container
    of writing fluid
  • **SNAPP** Word Cards
3. The environment:
  • well lit quiet room
	4. Position of the child:
	  • sitting cross legged in
	    front of writing surface
	    at least eight feet
	    from the front of the
	    SNAPPed card
	5. Number of repetitions:
	  • once per card
	  • repeat **SNAPP** without
	    cue
	6. How many times day/week:
	  • 3 times per week
	  • until concept is
	    mastered

Writing words begins with the child using words he already has in his oral spelling vocabulary. In written spelling, use the reading cards of one syllable that are three to five letters in length. Later he progresses to longer words that he has used for reading and oral spelling. Progressively the child will respond faster by writing the word as soon as possible after the card has been **SNAPP**ed. The child will begin to use a smaller and smaller writing instrument as his background is completed with 90% accuracy.

The child is seated on the floor with legs crossed, the writing surface centered on the floor in front of him. He holds a large marker or fat crayon entirely within his palm, with the palm of the other hand resting on the side of the writing surface. The adult says the word orally. The child writes the complete word on his writing surface.

Position for Writing

The sequence for written spelling is as follows:

1. Present the word as an oral spelling task.
2. Present the word as a written spelling task.
3. The child checks the word by reading and spelling it orally.

Example:
The adult says "When you read this word, say 'Ball, b a l l, ball'."
SNAPP the card, the child echoes loudly, "Ball, b a l l, ball."

Using the same card, give the child the following instruction:

"When you see this, make yours like mine, then read it and spell it aloud." **SNAPP** the card.

The child writes the word on the writing surface.
The child checks his word by using the oral spelling response aloud by saying, "Ball, b   a   l   l, ball."

If the child writes the word incorrectly he is either neurologically fatigued or is not ready for written spelling. If he makes mistake in spelling it aloud, he needs more oral spelling activity. If he reads it and spells it aloud correctly but has an error in writing it, he needs more of the Flashing Lights, Reading Silhouettes, and Pre-Writing **SNAPP** Cards. Change activity or return to Oral Spelling or to Three to Five Symbol Pre-Writing Cards.

The next step in developing the ability of the child to correctly write/spell words from his reading vocabulary is for the adult to dictate the word for the child to write it. The adult instructs the child: "When I say a word, you repeat the word, spell it aloud, repeat the word again, then write it. After you write it, read the word, spell it aloud, and then say the word again. The first word is _____ "

The child says the word, spells it aloud, repeats the word, and then writes it. He checks what he has written by reading the word, spelling it aloud, and saying the word again.

Developing control of large movements precedes developing control of fine movements. Ed Snapp [4.3]

The progression in the use of handwriting instruments goes from:
   the use of the palm
   the use of palm-held instrument
   the use of a wide tip marker or crayon held in palm
   the use of felt tip marker held with fingers while writing at
   a table
   the use of a pen or pencil.

Large movements (from the shoulder) made with large wide markers held in the palm of the hand are eventually replaced with smaller movements with smaller markers held in the loosely

146

flexed hand. The thumb rests against the middle finger while the wrist is slightly rotated outwardly. This results in the hand resting on the flexed third and fourth fingers.

Smaller print is the result of smaller movements with an even smaller marker ending with pen or pencil on paper held with the fingers.

References

4.1. *Dorland's Illustrated Medical Dictionary*, 24th Edition, p. 340, Publisher: W. B. Saunders Company, Philadelphia and London, 1965.

4.2. Snapp, Edward A., Jr., P. T., Notes from Workshop at SWTSU, 1977.

4.3. Snapp, Edward A., Jr., P. T., Quote from Graduate Courses held at TWU (1975) and SWTSU (1977).

CHRONOLOGY OF MATH

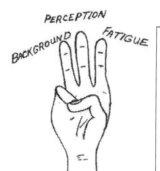

BACKGROUND: Stay within the child's developmental and educational background.

PERCEPTION: Stay within child's perceptual level for each of his senses.

FATIGUE: Stop before fatigue of the nervous system is apparent.

<u>SNAPP Principle</u>: Math operations can be taught developmentally by first presenting concrete information and then progressing to the abstraction of the operation.

"We begin by teaching Math as a language instead of teaching Math just as the manipulation of numerals. Consequently, it is more important to teach the concept of Math without writing." Ed Snapp. [5.1]

Math Chronology

All of the Math operations can be taught at each developmental level. For the targeted developmental levels of this book (up to 2nd grade) the curriculum includes addition and subtraction only. To present multiplication, division, fractions, geometry, and statistics in this book would be to go beyond a 2nd grader's BACKGROUND, PERCEPTION, and FATIGUE levels.

In this Chapter, Chronology of Math, the activities start with the most basic 1D (One Dimension) activities before progressing to more complex activities of 2D (Two Dimension) and 3D (Three

Dimension). Each 1D activity should be completed at a minimum of 90% accuracy before moving into any 2D activities. The same criteria apply to moving from 2D activities into 3D activities. Completion of 1D activities at the minimum of 90% accuracy provides a good foundation to building a better learner. Completion of any activity at a greater percentage of accuracy provides an even better foundation for your child to build upon to reach his potential. For more information on **SNAPP**'s Dimensions refer to **SNAPP**'s Dimensions on page 14 and to Dimensions listed in the Glossary or Appendix A.

The first level of Math (1D) employs concrete objects and rhythmic sounds in the child's environment. The second level (2D) employs **SNAPP** Cards with dots or rectangles that represent the concrete objects. The third level (3D) employs numerals used as numbers, and operational signs. The fourth level (4D), and the fifth level (5D) will not be completely dealt with in this book because they are appropriate for more advanced development (usually found in the older child).

The explanation of the following terms is given to help the reader understand their meanings as used in this chapter. The term "quantity" refers to the total number within a given group. The term "number" refers to the name given to a specific quantity, and the term "numeral" refers to the written symbol(s) for that quantity. Written numbers, regardless of the quantity, are represented by the ten numerals from 0 through 9. Our system of number notation uses a base of the ten numerals (0 through 9) that increase in value according to the column in which each numeral may be written.

Each of the steps in the following Chronology of Math is an important step and should not be omitted, no matter the age of your child. Do not take any step for granted. No steps can be omitted in the total sequence. Always begin at the beginning with what can be most easily grasped; that is, what is most concrete. In Math, a chair, a table, a ball, a cup, or a box can serve as a concrete object.

Recognition and Identification

A. Concrete Objects and Rhythmic Sounds (1D)

   1. Recognition of Objects (1D)

   Concept to be Learned: Recognition and Naming of Objects
   (Text Box 501)

1. Goal of exercise: • recognize an object as a single object • associate name with the object 2. What is needed: • assorted familiar objects 3. The environment: • natural lighting and temperature	4. Position of the child: • standing/walking 5. Number of repetitions: • as many as are required to touch, point, and name object(s) 6. How many times day/week: • 3 times per week • until concept is mastered

First, the Math environment is prepared by placing several items, familiar and known by the child, in the room. The adult demonstrates her recognition of an object, for example, by walking up to one chair, touching the chair with the palm of her hand and, while touching the chair, saying in a loud, clear voice, "Chair." She then says to the child, "Now you do it." The child then walks up to the chair, touches the chair and, while he is touching the chair, echoes in his loud, clear voice, "Chair." The adult then tells the child to walk to the other objects (that have been purposely placed), to touch them, one by one, and to name each one.

The next stage is to quickly name a particular object to which one is pointing. The adult demonstrates walking and standing directly in front of a table, for example, and then aggressively stretching her whole arm out toward the table and pointing directly at the table, quickly saying, "Table." The adult continues the demonstration by moving to stand directly in front of one object, and then another object taking the time to aggressively point, with arm fully extended, at that object and quickly naming it. The adult then says to the child, "Now you do it." Standing in front of an object and aggressively pointing at an object and quickly naming it works with the part of the brain associated with straight-line dominance.

2. Recognition of Number Concept by Pounding (1D) and Counting (2D)

Concept to be Learned: Recognition of Number Concept by Pounding (Text Box 502)

1. Goal of exercise: • match and join in pounding that is heard • echo the pounding heard • connect counting words with quantity or series of pounds heard • accurately pound the named quantity 2. What is needed: • hard surface or a drum 3. The environment: • dim to dark, quiet area	4. Position of the child: • lying face down (prone) where he cannot see adult's pounding hand 5. Number of repetitions: • up to 5 repetitions 6. How many times day/week: • 3 times per week • until concept is mastered

Pounding helps a child understand single quantity concepts, or the number of a given quantity. It also helps teach sequencing concepts that are critical in the understanding of Math.

Assuming that the child can hear, he lies face down on the floor in a dimly lit room in a position and location that prevents him from being able to see the adult's pounding arm and hand. The child's sensory input is limited to the sound and possibly the vibration of the adult's pounding.

The adult starts by pounding a slow, even rhythm, pounding one beat per second, and tells the child, "Pound with me." The child joins in and does pounding that matches the steady rhythm of the adult's pounding.

This palm pounding activity progresses over time to include the adult presentation of **steady** rhythms of varying lengths and of different speeds. It may take several trials for the child to echo the correct single pound or multiple pounds. For example, if the adult pounds twice, the child may pound several times more than twice because to some children two means something more than one, not necessarily just two. In the event of an error, the adult does not verbally correct the child; instead the adult says, "Let's do that again. Listen." If the child is not accurate the second time, change to another activity and return to this activity at a later time. The child may not be ready for this activity, in which case he continues with the steady rhythm activity.

After the child matches each of the adult's presentation of several different steady palm pounding rhythms, the adult, says to the child, "Listen." The adult pounds **once** on a surface with her **fist** (the little finger side of the fist), then tells the child, "Now you do it." The child echoes what he hears with a single pound of his **fist** on the surface. The adult listens for the correct echo response.

Variations of pounding sounds may be made by hitting the fist on the floor, or hitting the fist into the palm of the hand, or using a drumbeat.

3. Pounding and Counting (2D)

The adult tells the child "Listen" then demonstrates by simultaneously pounding out and counting out loud a single pounding or a random number of poundings up to and including five then tells the child, "Now you do it." The child echoes with the same number of beats, counting as he pounds. The adult tells the child "Listen!" and demonstrates the pounding and counting of another quantity and says, "Now you do it", and the child echoes with the same number of beats, counting as he pounds.

Later, any number up to and including ten is simultaneously pounded out and counted out loud by the adult. The child then echoes it.

When the sequence of echoing is mastered, the adult and child count together as they pound each beat. Example: The adult says "Now we will pound and count to five together," and pounds in the same steady rhythm.

As lesser quantity numbers are mastered, the adult and child pound and count together to random numbers under ten, then to random numbers under twenty.

Later, other forms of steady rhythm that may be used include beating on a drum, marching feet on a hard floor, marching to music, or clapping hands to the steady rhythm of music or nursery rhymes. Math and music complement each other. Any variety of large contact sounds with movement will result in whole body involvement.

4. Matching Varied Rhythms (2D)

For matched rhythm pounding, the adult tells the child, "Listen!" and pounds out a rhythm; for example, pound, pause, pound, pound, pound (pound once, pause, pound three times). She then tells the child, "Now you do it." The child

154

then echoes the same rhythm. Other rhythm combinations can be used such as: pound twice, pause, pound four times; pound three times, pause, pound three times; or two steady pounds followed by three fast pounds.

The child is ready to move on when he can successfully distinguish between one object and multiple objects, between one pound and multiple poundings and when he can successfully match various rhythmic poundings.

5. Echoing Counting of LARGE Objects within a Group (2D)

Concept to be Learned: Counting of Large Objects (Text Box 503)

1. Goal of exercise: • recognize total quantity within a group by counting each object • group of large objects that are alike 2. What is needed: • assorted familiar objects 3. The environment: • natural lighting and temperature	4. Position of the child: • standing/walking • point with large arm gestures 5. Number of repetitions: • 3 repetitions at random for each quantity (10-0) 6. How many times day/ week: • 3 times per week • until concept is mastered

The adult models identifying two and/or three of the same kind of object by touching each of the objects and saying the corresponding number and naming the object. For example, 1 chair, 2 chairs, 3 chairs. Then have the child repeat this action by telling him, "Now you do it." This lets the child know that numbers represent objects. The adult continues to demonstrate this activity by having more than one of several types of objects in the room, and using the different objects for different demonstrations. The quantity of each type of object should vary, so that different quantities are presented.

6. Independent Counting of LARGE Objects within a Group (2D)

The adult uses several like-objects to form a group of five or fewer. She begins the demonstration by stating, "I am going to count the number of chairs in this group." She touches each chair in the group as she states "One chair, two chairs, . . ." until all the chairs in the group are touched and counted. She then states, "There are ___ chairs in this group."

After this demonstration the child is told, "Now you count the chairs in the group." The child touches each chair with the palm of his hand and states the number and the name of the object. For example, the child touches each chair and counts, "One chair, two chairs. There are two chairs in this group." After the child counts the number of chairs in a group of chairs correctly, the adult says, "Yes, there are two chairs in the group." This hands-on activity is repeated with different sized groups of like objects to strengthen and build areas of the brain associated with sequencing and naming like objects in a group.

After many successful experiences of touching and sequentially counting like objects in a group, the adult and child move back away from a certain group of like objects. The adult then demonstrates the next activity of sequentially counting LARGE objects within a group from a distance. For example, the adult aggressively points to each chair of a group of two chairs and loudly counts, "One chair, two chairs," and then states, "Yes, there are two chairs in this group." Then the child is told, "Now you do it." After the child completes aggressively pointing and loudly counting, "One chair, two chairs," he turns to the adult and states, "Yes, there are two chairs in this group."

Repetition of this far point sequential counting activity, encompassing verbal verification of the quantity of items, strengthens the areas of the brain associated with far point sequential counting and strengthens the areas of the brain associated with an awareness of parts of a whole.

7. Estimating Quantity (2D)

Estimation is the ability to quantify the total number of objects in a group of like items without first sequentially counting each item. Estimation is a visual activity as well as a Math concept. The group being estimated must be made up of clearly visible and clearly separated like items that are grouped away from any other like objects in the room. Solid black objects, such as coffee can lids, blocks, balled up socks, and/or other solid colored objects (except for rolling balls) on a light colored floor make for a good visual contrast. To aid in visually contrasting the group of like items to be estimated from the surface of the floor and/or to maintain the child's attention, a lamp can be focused on the objects to be estimated.

Concept to be Learned: Estimation of Quantity within a Group (2D) (Text Box 504)

1. Goal of exercise: • estimate a quantity of objects within groups • after estimating, verifying quantity by counting each item aloud 2. What is needed: • groups of like objects • bright light (optional) 3. The environment: • natural lighting and temperature • surface with high color contrast with objects used	4. Position of the child: • sitting/standing/ walking 5. Number of repetitions: • 3 repetitions, quantities at random 6. How many times day/ week: • 3 times per week • until concept is mastered

The adult sits across from the child and places, for example, three blue beanbags in a group between herself and the child. The adult says, "I estimate there are three beanbags in this group. I will verify my estimation by counting the beanbags." The adult then points to each beanbag and counts it. "One beanbag, two beanbags, three beanbags." She then says, "Yes, there are three beanbags in this group."

The adult tells the child to cover his eyes or to look away because if the child watches the adult change the number of beanbags in the group, he may be counting them. While the child covers his eyes or looks away, the adult, for example, places two beanbags between them. She tells the child to look at the group of beanbags and say his estimation. The child responds, "I estimate there are two beanbags in this group. I will verify my estimation by counting the beanbags." The child then counts, "One beanbag, two beanbags. Yes, there are two beanbags in this group."

Continue this estimation activity by changing the number of beanbags in the group from one to five while the child covers his eyes or looks away. Each time the child estimates the number of beanbags in the group, he then verifies his estimation by individually counting each beanbag. Eventually, the child should instantaneously and correctly estimate any number of like objects in a group containing from one to ten objects.

A child will discover if he is incorrect in his estimation when he counts for verification. He does not need to be told he is incorrect! He will know it! Ed Snapp sometimes used the activity of shooting a basket as an example of when someone does not need to be told something he can realize on his own. Yet, how many times when a basket is missed someone says, "You missed." Remember, if a mistake is made, the child's background of understanding of a concept is exceeded and/or his nervous system is fatigued which may, in this case, cause errors in perception. Regardless of the cause of mistakes, make a change to a lower developmental Math activity or change to an activity in another subject area.

When you and your child are on an outing take advantage of any opportunity for your child to estimate a number of like objects, such as seven birds on a wire, or six tables in front of the restaurant, or nine people in front of you in the check-out line.

8. Introducing the Concept of 0 (Zero) (1D)

Concept to be Learned: Introducing the Concept of 0 (Zero) (Text Box 505)

1. Goal of exercise: • recognize absence of objects • count no objects 2. What is needed: • room with various types of objects 3. The environment: • well lit room; spotlight optional	4. Position of the child: • standing by adult 5. Number of repetitions: • as needed 6. How many times day/ week: • 3 times per week • until concept is mastered

To introduce the concept of "zero", include a group with no object present. For example, adult says, "Tell me, how many elephants are in the room." "There are no elephants in the room," or "There aren't any," or "I don't see any elephants" are examples of acceptable responses. The adult then responds, "Yes, there are zero elephants in the room."

Continue using other clear examples of zero objects for the child to respond: "There are zero (names the object of concern) in the room/area." When the child's responses demonstrate that he has a clear understanding of zero, it is then appropriate to include groups of objects that vary in quantity from zero to ten when working on estimation.

To extend the concept of zero to previously counted objects in the room, the adult removes all of a previously counted item from the area used for grouping and states, "There are now zero (name the objects) in the area."

B. Recognition of Quantities Using **SNAPP** Dot Cards (1D)

Concept to be Learned: Naming a Group of Dots (Text Box 506)

1. Goal of exercise:
  • recognize quantity of dots on a **SNAPP**ed card
  • name quantity of dots on the Cards
2. What is needed:
  • prepared **SNAPP** Dot Cards
  • spotlight optional
3. The environment:
  • well lit room
  • dimly lit room if spot light used
	4. Position of the child:
	  • seated on floor, crossed legs
	  • 8 feet or more in front of adult
	5. Number of repetitions:
	  • **SNAPP** card 3 times with prompt
	  • **SNAPP** card 3 times w/ out prompt
	  • if inaccurate without prompt set card aside to re-present later
	6. How many times day/week:
	  • 3 times per week
	  • until concept is mastered

Here are some examples of **SNAPP** Dot Cards:

This card is read

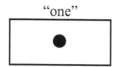

These cards are read

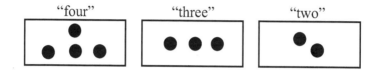

These cards are read

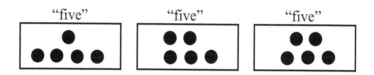

SNAPP Dot Cards (cards with groups of solid black dots located in the middle of a **SNAPP** Card) are used to teach the child recognition of a quantity and the name for that quantity. Present Dot Cards with the different quantities in random order rather than presenting them in sequential order. Dots on a card represent objects. **SNAPP** Dot Cards are the transitional abstract link from objects to numbers just like silhouettes are the transitional abstract link from a concrete object to a word.

Usually dots the size of a quarter can be easily read from the distance of eight to ten feet. Greater viewing distances will require larger sized dots (and consequently different size cards) and probably greater separation between the dots. You may need to experiment with different size dots to determine what the child requires to effectively read **SNAPP** Dot Cards.

Early in the learning process, dots should be in a random pattern in the middle of a card rather than displayed in domino style, which might be a familiar pattern. Some cards will form a different pattern when turned upside down. Variations of card patterns should be used. For example, for "four dots" there can be a vertical pattern, a horizontal pattern, a group of three and one, or a random pattern. In the variations, a domino pattern may be used as long as it is not the only pattern.

In a dominant, loud voice, the adult says to the child, "When you see this say, 'Three'." The adult then **SNAPP**s the "three" card, and the child immediately says, "Three" in a dominant, loud voice. Repeat the **SNAPP**ing of the card without the verbal teaching cue. If the child cannot identify the information on the card without the verbal cue, he has not mastered that Math fact. It must be re-taught, complete with the verbal cue.

Next say to the child, "When you see this say, "One." The adult **SNAPP**s the Dot Card containing one dot. The child then says, "One." Repeat the **SNAPP**ing of the card without the verbal teaching cue.

Then say to the child "I am going to mix up these cards and I will **SNAPP** either the Dot Card with one dot or the Dot Card with three dots. Tell me what you see." The adult then **SNAPP**s one card and the child responds. If the child's response is correct, **SNAPP** the other card. Repeat the **SNAPP**ing of the cards without the verbal teaching cue. When the child is consistent with correctly responding to the Dot Card with one dot, two dots, and three dots, introduce **SNAPP** Dot Cards with patterns of four or more dots.

If the child cannot identify the information on the **SNAPP** Dot Cards without the verbal cue, have the child move farther away from the card and repeat the **SNAPP**. Do not slow down the **SNAPP**ing of the card. **SNAPP** the card again! If he does not correctly verbalize the **SNAPP** Dot Card information, he may need additional time on independent counting of LARGE

Objects within a Group (See page 155) or Estimating Quantity (See page 157) before working with **SNAPP** Dot Cards.

If the child does not perceive that there are dots on the card, he may need more time with the visual activity of Contrasting Dark and Light (See page 75) as well as more experience with Silhouette Cards (See page 115) to complete the child's developmental background. Focusing a spotlight on the **SNAPP**ed card can also aid the child in perceiving what is on the card.

Errors may indicate that the material is exceeding the child's developmental background, and/or he has begun to become neurologically fatigued. Change the activity! (See Varied Activities on page 109.)

At a later time present **SNAPP** Dot Cards again. If the error is repeated he has exceeded his developmental background. He must again experience simpler Math concepts before proceeding.

Remember, even wrong answers are recorded in the brain. That is why we stop and change to another activity before neurological fatigue occurs.

After the child can properly respond to all **SNAPP** Dot Cards up to five, add a card representing the concept of 0, a card that contains no dots. The **SNAPP** Zero Card is a blank card that is presented only after the child correctly identifies the quantity on each of the **SNAPP** Dot Cards presented without any having to be re-taught. Say to the child, "When you see this, say 'Zero'." The adult then **SNAPP**s the Zero Card. The child responds by saying "Zero."

This card is read

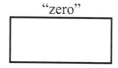

"zero"

When a child consistently identifies the quantity of grouped dots and when he consistently recognizes the **SNAPP** Zero Card, he is then ready to learn to recognize and label the written numerals.

C. Recognition of Numerals (1D)

A numeral is the written symbol for a quantity. There are only ten numerals, 0 through 9. These numerals are used to write all numbers. The number value of a given numeral depends upon which column it appears or is placed in; that is, whether it represents units, tens, hundreds, or greater quantities.

1. Naming Numbers from **SNAPP** Numeral Cards (1D)

    Concept to be Learned: Naming Numbers from **SNAPP** Numeral Cards (Text Box 507)

1. Goal of exercise: • recognize numerals presented on **SNAPP** Cards • name numerals presented on **SNAPP** Cards 2. What is needed: • prepared **SNAPP** Numeral Cards • spot light optional 3. The environment: • well lit room • dimly lit if spot light used	4. Position of the child: • seated on floor, crossed legs 8 feet or more in front of adult 5. Number of repetitions: • **SNAPP** card 3 times with prompt • **SNAPP** card 3 times w/out prompt • if inaccurate without prompt set card aside to present later 6. How many times day/ week: • 3 times per week • until concept is mastered

For **SNAPP** Numeral Card activity the child sits cross-legged on the floor at a distance of eight feet or more from the adult.

Good posture with the trunk erect and not slumped should always be stressed. A slumped trunk indicates that this part of the body has become neurologically fatigued. The activity and the position of the body should be changed, without comment, if poor posture is observed.

If physical fatigue and/or neurological fatigue are apparent, change to activities by selecting one or more of the Examples of Varied Learning Activities listed on page 109.

These cards are read

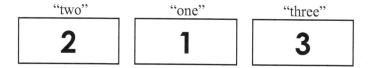

"two" "one" "three"

2 1 3

The adult starts with the **SNAPP** Numeral Cards 1, 2, and 3, in random order in her hands and says to the child, "When you see this say 'Two'," then **SNAPP**s the two card. The child says, "Two." Then the adult says to the child, "When you see this say 'One', "then **SNAPP**s the one card." The child says, "One." The adult presents, in this manner, all three of the **SNAPP** Numeral Cards in random order until the child correctly responds to the numerals 1, 2, and 3. The adult then presents these **SNAPP** Numeral Cards, in random order, with no verbal cue given other than the initial instruction, "Tell me what you see."

The adult presents all of the **SNAPP** Numeral Cards in a random order in this manner until all the numerals, 0 through 9, are correctly responded to by the child. As the child becomes competent, include Numeral Cards with higher numbers through 19.

2. Writing Numerals from **SNAPP** Numeral Cards (2D)

Concept to be Learned: Writing Numerals from **SNAPP** Numeral Cards (Text Box 508)

1. Goal of exercise: • accurately write the numeral shown 2. What is needed: • prepared **SNAPP** Numeral Cards • writing materials • writing surface 3. The environment: • well lit room, optional spot light focused on card 4. Position of the child: • seated on floor, crossed legs	• 8 feet or more in front of adult • in front of writing surface 5. Number of repetitions: • **SNAPP** card 3 times with prompt • **SNAPP** card 3 times w/ out prompt • if inaccurate without prompt present at a later time 6. How many times day/week: • 3 times per week • until concept is mastered

The numerals have already been introduced as a naming or reading activity. The same cards will be used to present the numerals as a writing activity.

A child sits cross-legged on the floor with the writing equipment near him, and writes on a marker board or paper that is centered on the floor in front of him. The child places his non-writing hand on the board to steady it. The writing instrument is held *within* his palm and he writes with his arm extended. Movements to write originate in the shoulder and the elbow.

The adult says, "When you see this, write what you see." The adult **SNAPP**s a Numeral Card. The child writes what he sees. An immediate and correct response is required! In this case, the correct written response.

166

Watch for signs of neurological fatigue. Keep lessons short. Look for mistakes, restlessness, inability to maintain focus on the task, or the child's trunk beginning to slump—for these indicate neurological fatigue. Change the learning activity often to avoid fatigue. (See Varied Learning Activities on page 109.)

Addition

A solid understanding of quantification and writing of numbers is necessary before addition can be introduced. The child begins addition by combining groups of real objects. He will progress to split-group addition on **SNAPP** Cards with solid dots, and written numerals. And finally he will progress to addition of numbers on **SNAPP** Cards.

A. Addition with Real Objects (2D)

Concept to be Learned: Addition of Groups of Objects
(Text Box 509)

1. Goal of exercise: • accurately add together groups of like objects 2. What is needed: • two groups of like objects 3. The environment: • well lit room; work surface with color contrast to objects used 4. Position of the child: • standing or sitting near prepared groups of objects	5. Number of repetitions: • until accurate with prompt • until accurate without prompt • if inaccurate w/out prompt re-present at a later time • if second error, re-present later 6. How many times day/week: • 3 times per week • until concept is mastered

The child starts with any number of real objects in a group totaling five or less.

Show the child two groups of real objects such as boxes; the first group for example, has one box, the other has two boxes. Say to the child, "I need to count each group separately. One box. This group has 1 box." Walk to the next group, point to each box and count them aloud, and say, "One box, two boxes. This group has 2 boxes." Then move one or both groups to form a single, larger group, and recount them. Say to the child. "Now I will count the larger group I have when I add them together. One box, two boxes, three boxes. The larger group now has 3 boxes." The adult replaces the boxes to their original positions and tells the child, "Now you do it." Repeat this activity using up to 10 objects.

When the child can successfully recognize the total number of objects in a combined group, and recognize it as a new, larger group with the new quantity, he is ready to move to a higher concept of an oral addition sentence by introducing the word "plus".

Say to the child, "The **word 'plus'** means that we are adding one quantity to another quantity to create a new, larger total quantity." Be sure that the child understands that "plus" indicates adding (joining) one number quantity to the other number quantity. At this point, the "+" Symbol Card should be made and added to the **SNAPP** reading/writing cards.

Using the same groups of objects as above, one group of one objects and one group of two objects, the adult demonstrates to the child as before, but simultaneously says the word "plus" as she moves the group(s) together to create the new larger group of three. Example, the adult says, "One box (pointing to the group of 1) **plus** (while moving one or both groups to create the new larger group) two boxes, three boxes."

The boxes are again placed in the original groups of one group of one box and one group of two boxes and the child is told; "Now you do it." The child then counts as he moves the group(s) saying as he counts, "One box, plus two boxes, three boxes."

Now that the quantity is known, the adult states, "Three boxes, one box plus two boxes, three boxes. Now you tell me." The child states, "Three boxes, one box plus two boxes, three boxes."

When the child is proficient in adding objects, the adult then demonstrates the next step by not naming the object(s) as they are combined. Example: "three, one plus two, three". After the objects are replaced in the original groups, the child does similarly as he echoes the teaching demonstration, "Three, one plus two, three."

When he can recognize small groups of objects, increase the number of objects in the two groups to a total of ten.

Always require 90% accuracy. When he performs with less than 90% accuracy he may have exceeded his developmental background; in which case he requires more background of the prior levels of developmental activities. Or perhaps he has become neurologically fatigued and is beginning to make mistakes after having been successful. In this case change the activity.

B. Addition with Split-dot **SNAPP** Cards (3D)

Concept to be Learned: Addition with Split-dot **SNAPP** Cards (Text Box 510)

1. Goal of exercise: • recognize total of two split-dot groups • name total of two split-dot groups 2. What is needed: • **SNAPP** Addition Split-dot Cards 3. The environment: • well lit room or dimly lit if spot light is used 4. Position of the child: • seated on floor, crossed legs • 8 feet or more in front of adult	5. Number of repetitions: • **SNAPP** card 3 times with prompt • **SNAPP** card 3 times w/ out prompt • if inaccurate without prompt present at a later time 6. How many times day/week: • 3 times per week • until concept is mastered

As the child is successful with real objects, **SNAPP** Cards containing split-dot groups for addition are introduced and taught. Be sure to tell the child the sum of each combination on the card when teaching recognition of and the name of the quantity before he is expected to respond. Saying the number of dots on the card names that card and teaches the child the language used for that quantity.

The adult says, "When you see this, say, 'Five'," (the sum of the number of dots on the card that is the total of the two groups of dots on the card), then **SNAPP** the card. The child echoes that number.

Start with two groups of dots on the card totaling five or less. Say to the child: "When you see this, say 'five'." **SNAPP** the card and the child says, "Five." Responding with the total amount only is a simpler concept (labeling) than naming the two groups and the total on the card (a Math sentence), which will be presented later.

This card is read

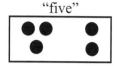

This card can be rotated 180 degrees for a new combination that is also read "five." The commutative property of addition is thus presented. "Commutative property" means the order of the addends does not matter; the answer is still the same (whether it is "two plus three" or "three plus two").

This card is read

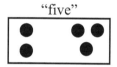

When the child can successfully echo the total number of dots on a **SNAPP** Card, have him respond to the **SNAPP**ed card by saying the total number without being taught or prompted each time. At this stage he is independently recognizing and identifying the sum or total number of dots on the card. Present the cards in random order.

If a child volunteers the observation that there are two groups on the card, and names the quantity of each group, he has demonstrated that he is ready for the next step.

Accurate responses are required. Remember, quick responses enhance decisiveness, confidence and dominance.

When the child is successful with the total for two groups of dots, and using the same Dot Cards, say to the child, "When you see this, say, 'Five, two plus three, five'." The child reads the **SNAPP**ed Card and echoes, "Five, two plus three, five."

This card is now read

"five, two plus three, five"

When the child can successfully echo total, first group plus second group, total, have him respond to a **SNAPP** Card dot addition without being cued. This transition may be made immediately after teaching the card (the echo stage). New presentations at one time, however, are limited to three cards before trying the transition. For the transition, present in random order the cards whose quantity labels have just been taught. If a mistake occurs, set aside that card to re-teach at a later session or to present again to see if an error occurs again. The first error may have been caused by neurological fatigue.

Accurate responses are required. Remember, quick responses enhance decisiveness, confidence, and dominance.

Using Split-dot Cards will help the child move from real objects to abstract numbers.

This card is now read

"six, three plus three, six"

C. Addition with Numbers (3D)

We are now ready to advance to the next level using numerals and operational symbols instead of just dots.

Presenting The Operational Symbol "+" (plus)

The "+" (plus) word and its concept have already been used (See page 168) when combining groups of objects with the **SNAPP** Split-dot Addition Cards.

The "+" Symbol Card should be made and added to the **SNAPP** Cards. The name of the plus Symbol Card is now introduced when using Number Cards as follows:

While holding the plus card in the position to be **SNAPP**ed, the adult says, "When you see this, say 'Plus'," then **SNAPP**s the card. The child says, "Plus."

This card is read

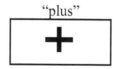

After mastering the reading of the "plus" operational symbol, it is presented as a writing task. The child is seated with crossed legs, with his writing equipment on the floor centered in front of him, holding the writing instrument within the palm of his preferred hand.

While holding the card in the proper position for rotating, the adult says, "When you see this, make yours like mine," then **SNAPP**s the card. The child's response is to write the "+" on his writing paper.

Concept to be Learned: Addition with Numbers (1D) (Text Box 511)

1. Goal of exercise:
   - accurately identify the numbers, and operational sign
   - name total on the **SNAPP** Cards
2. What is needed:
   - **SNAPP** Addition Cards
3. The environment:
   - well lit room or dimly lit if spot light is used
4. Position of the child:
   - seated on floor, crossed legs
   - 8 feet or more in front of adult
5. Number of repetitions:
   - **SNAPP** card 3 times with prompt
   - **SNAPP** card 3 times w/out prompt
   - if inaccurate without prompt re-present at a later time
6. How many times day/week:
   - 3 times per week
   - until concept is mastered

SNAPP Cards using numerals with addition up to a total of ten are introduced. The recognition of a two number adding combination (2 + 1) is understood to represent a specific value (3), and becomes an "addition fact." Introduce **SNAPP** Cards of small values first in random order, working up to larger values.

The following is how to present a **SNAPP** Addition Card used for addition of numbers. Say to the child, "When you see this, say 'Three'" and then **SNAPP** the card. The child echoes "Three."

These cards are read

"three"

$$2 + 1$$

"two"   "five"

When the child is successful with the total for two groups of numbers, and using the same cards, say to the child, "When you see this, say, 'Five, three plus two, five'." The child reads the **SNAPP**ed card and echoes, "Five, three plus two, five."

This card is now read

"five, three plus two, five"

3 + 2

"Always say the total first because that's what we want them to see, when they begin to see problems, we want them to see answers not the problems and if you always say three plus two, five, you always see it as a problem. But if you always see three plus two as "five" then you have the answer as soon as you look at it. That's the way we want the children to handle it." Ed Snapp [(5.2)]

Several additional teaching examples will be necessary for the child to become proficient in this activity. Continue by **SNAPP**ing previously learned cards as the child independently states the addition Math sentence without being prompted or re-taught.

Accurate responses are required. Remember, quick responses enhance decisiveness, confidence and dominance.

Subtraction

A solid understanding of quantity and basic addition is necessary before subtraction can be introduced. Real objects are used first to learn both the concept and the Math language of subtraction.

A. Subtraction with Real Objects (3D)

Concept to be Learned: Subtraction with Real Objects (2D) (Text Box 512)

1. Goal of exercise: • recognize initial quantity • remove a given quantity • accurately identify remaining quantity 2. What is needed: • groups of objects of needed quantity 3. The environment: • well lit room; work surface with color contrast to objects used 4. Position of the child: • standing or sitting near prepared groups of objects	5. Number of repetitions: • if accurate, proceed to next group • if error made, present again • if second error, re-present later 6. How many times day/week: • 3 times per week • until concept is mastered

The child starts with any number of real objects in a group totaling five or fewer.

Show the child a group of real objects, example: five boxes. Say to the child, "Five boxes." The child echoes, "Five boxes." Remove three of the boxes while saying to the child, "Three boxes are taken away." Return to the remaining boxes and say, "Two boxes remain." Recreate the beginning group of boxes for him to repeat what he has seen and heard. Then say to the child, "Now you do it." The child echoes, "Five boxes. Three boxes are taken away. Two boxes remain." Vary this activity by starting with a different number of boxes or taking a different number of boxes away. This activity can also be done working with plastic coffee can lids, beanbags or other easily handled objects.

When the child can successfully recognize how many objects remain in a group, and recognize it as a new, smaller group with a lesser quantity, he is ready to move to a higher concept of an oral subtraction sentence by introducing the **word "minus"**. Say to the child, "The word 'minus' means that we are taking away one quantity from another quantity to create a new, smaller quantity."

Using the same groups of five boxes as in the subtraction problem above, the adult demonstrates to the child as before, but simultaneously says the word "minus" as she removes three of the boxes to create the new smaller group of two boxes. Example, the adult says, "Five boxes (pointing to the group of 5 boxes) minus (while removing three of the boxes to create the new smaller group) three boxes, two boxes remain." To reinforce this concept, say to the child, "The word 'minus' means that we are taking away one quantity from a larger quantity to create a remaining quantity."

When the child can successfully identify how many objects remain, without being prompted or re-taught, increase the number of objects in the group up to a total of nine.

For the child to be able to do this activity independently, after preparing a group of five, tell the child, "Show me three boxes, five boxes minus two boxes, three boxes." When the child carries out the activity without error advance to the next level, where the objects are not named. For example, "Three, five minus two, three" without naming the objects. The child completes the same actions, then echoes, "Three, five minus two, three."

Always require 90% accuracy. When the child cannot achieve 90% accuracy it indicates fatigue and/or he has not yet completed the necessary background and needs to go back to an earlier developmental level of Math.

B. **SNAPP** Dot Subtraction Cards (2D)

After the child is successful with real objects, he then progresses to split-group subtraction on **SNAPP** Cards with solid and empty dots. On the Dot Subtraction Card, the hollow dots represent the part that is taken away (the subtrahend) from the larger beginning quantity (the minuend) that includes both the hollow and solid dots. What is left (the solid black dots) is the answer (the remainder).

The following is an example of a **SNAPP** Split-dot Subtraction Card.

Concept to be Learned: Subtraction with Split-dot **SNAPP** Cards (2D) (Text Box 513)

1. Goal of exercise: • recognize empty dots are subtracted quantity, solid dots are remaining quantity, • accurately state remainder 2. What is needed: • **SNAPP** Split-dot Subtraction Cards 3. The environment: • well lit room or dimly lit if spot light is used 4. Position of the child: • seated on floor, crossed legs	• 8 feet or more in front of adult 5. Number of repetitions: • **SNAPP** card 3 times with prompt • **SNAPP** card 3 times w/ out prompt • if inaccurate without prompt re-present at a later time 6. How many times day/week: • 3 times per week • until concept is mastered

178

Be sure to teach the child each card's subtraction language before the card is **SNAPP**ed and a response is expected. The teaching pattern and response is the remainder (the answer), which is the number of solid black dots on the card.

Accurate responses are required. Remember, quick responses enhance decisiveness, confidence and dominance.

This card is read

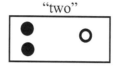

Say to the child: "When you see this, say two." **SNAPP** the card and the child says, "Two." Or say to the child, "When you see this, write 2." **SNAPP** the card and the child writes 2.

Using Subtraction Cards will help the child move from real objects to abstract numbers. Responding with the remainder is a simpler concept (labeling) than naming the total group, the group that is taken away and the remainder on the card (a Math sentence).

The following cards are examples of how **SNAPP** Cards are read.

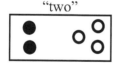   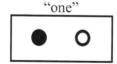

When the child can successfully echo the remainder of dots on a card, have him respond to the **SNAPP**ed card by saying the remainder without being prompted or re-taught. The cards are presented in random order.

If there is an error, set the card aside to be re-presented at a later time. If an error is made at the re-presentation he may be neurologically fatigued or may need more of the earlier developmental experiences in either Math or flashing lights, or both.

Accurate responses are required. Remember, quick responses enhance decisiveness, confidence and dominance.

When the child is successful with the remainder using the **SNAPP** Dot Subtraction Cards, introduce the oral subtraction sentence. The **SNAPP** Dot Subtraction Cards differ from the **SNAPP** Dot Addition Cards because Snapp had the total given first instead of the answer. He did this because some of the children just looked for the detail of the solid dots (the answer) and not the whole card. So, with the **SNAPP** Dot Subtraction Cards, tell the child, "When you see this, say, "Five minus three is two." **SNAPP** the card! The child echoes "Five minus three is two." When it is a writing activity, tell the child, "When you see this, write 5-3=2

This card is now read

"five minus three, is two"

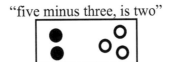

Always require 90% accuracy. When the child cannot achieve 90% accuracy it indicates fatigue and/or he has not yet completed the necessary background and needs to go back to an earlier developmental level of Math.

C. Subtraction with Numbers (3D)

At this level the child subtracts numbers on **SNAPP** Cards and states the full subtraction sentence.

Prior to this level the ten numerals (0 through 9) have had their names taught as reading activities ("When you see this, say __,") and have been taught as a writing activity ("When you see this, make yours like mine.") At this level the "numerals" become "numbers" because they represent the named quantity. Once it is used to indicate a given quantity, it is a number!

The Operational Symbol "—" (Minus)

The "—" (minus) word has already been presented in an earlier subtraction section (See page 177). The name of the Symbol Card "—" (minus) is introduced when using Number Cards and should be included to the **SNAPP** Cards.

The minus Symbol Card is introduced as follows. While holding the minus card in the position to be **SNAPP**ed the adult says, "When you see this, say 'Minus'," then **SNAPP**s the card. The child says, "Minus."

This card is read

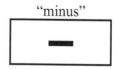
"minus"

After mastering the reading of the "—" operational symbol, it is presented as a writing task.

While holding the card in the proper position for rotating, the adult says to the child, "When you see this, make your minus symbol like mine," then **SNAPP**s the card. The child's response is to write the "—" on his writing paper.

Be sure that the child understands that the "—" (minus) on the **SNAPP Card** indicates subtracting (deducting) one number (quantity) on the card from the other number (quantity) on the card. The larger number on the card (the minuend) minus the smaller number on the card (the subtrahend) gives the answer (the remainder), the number of objects from the original group that remain.

Say to the child "The word 'minus' means that we are taking away one quantity from another quantity to create a remaining quantity."

Concept to be Learned: Subtraction with Numbers (3D) (Text Box 514)

1. Goal of exercise: • accurately state the math sentence 2. What is needed: • **SNAPP** Subtraction Cards 3. The environment: • well lit room or dimly lit if spot light is used 4. Position of the child: • seated on floor, crossed legs • 8 feet or more in front of adult	5. Number of repetitions: • **SNAPP** card 3 times with prompt • **SNAPP** card 3 times w/ out prompt • if inaccurate without prompt re-present at a later time 6. How many times day/week: • 3 times per week or • until concept is mastered

SNAPP Cards using subtraction from numbers less than ten are introduced. The recognition of a two number subtraction combination (3-2) is understood as representing, or being equal to a specific value—named one (1) in this case. Start by introducing small values first in random order, and then work up to larger values.

The following is how to present a **SNAPP** Card used for subtracting numbers. Say to the child, "When you see this say, 'One'." **SNAPP** the card! The child echoes, "One."

These cards are read

"one"

3-2

"four"

5-1

This activity continues, using the same **SNAPP** Cards, with the child independently naming the remainder as each Subtraction Card is **SNAPP**ed. If the child is unable to name the remainder independently, he has not learned the given task. He must return to earlier activities, whether in Math or visual development.

Remember, quick responses enhance dominance, confidence, and decisiveness. Accurate responses are required.

When the child is successful with the remainder using **SNAPP** Number Cards, introduce the subtraction sequence. Say to the child just before the card is **SNAPP**ed, "When you see this say, 'One, three minus two, one'." The child reads the card and echoes "One, three minus two, one."

These cards are read

"one, three minus two, one"

3-2

"two, five minus three, two"

5-3

Conclusion

This concludes our presentations of Math. Snapp presented ways of multiplication, division, fractions and decimals but we are concluding this chapter with subtraction. We think a child of the ages for which this book is intended should fully experience addition and subtraction not only with "book learning" but with his life's experiences, as well. Addition and Subtraction are basic to mathematics.

Throughout the day there are numerous ways at home for your child, of first or second grade, to handle Math while "building" his appreciation, abilities, and Math language in addition and subtraction. These numerous opportunities can include:
- Stating facts
- Naming objects
- Counting objects
- Grouping like objects
- Repeated grouping of same quantity
- Repeated addition of the same quantity
- Repeated subtraction of the same quantity from a larger given quantity

There are different opportunities for the child to employ Math concepts at home. For instance: determining the number of settings for a table, separating to create equal shares of food items, helping to cook from recipes, and helping out around the house.

Some examples:

- The adult says, "We will need to set the table for our family of 5 people. Each person needs 1 fork. So please take 5 forks out of the drawer."

- The adult says, "There will be our family plus Aunt Jane's family here for supper. There are 5 people in our family, and 4 people in her family. We will need 9 spoons in all. Please put 9 spoons on the table."

- The adult says, "We have 12 pieces of candy for you 4 children to share. Let's see how many pieces each of you will receive. One for Sally, one for you, one for Jim, one for John. Then another one for Sally, another for you, another for Jim, another for John." (This continues until all the pieces of candy are assigned equally). "Now let's count how many pieces of candy each of you will receive." Then the adult states, "So, each of you will receive 3 pieces of candy."

- The adult says, "We folded a lot of towels when we took the laundry out of the dryer. Let's count how many towels we folded in all."

These examples of "stories" are of the sort that the child will experience in real life and will experience in any Math curriculum. Real-life situations are helpful in the transition from the concrete "hands on" experiences to the abstract stories found in Math textbooks.

Purposely employing Math in the child's home provides him with life experiences that will build Math language and concepts. The results will be reinforcement, expansion, and strengthening of his background in Math to better prepare for acquiring multiplication, division, fractions, decimals and beyond.

> **"No kind of acceleration is an advantage unless you have finished everything that comes up to it. We have to finish background functions." Ed Snapp, Pflugerville, Texas CCDE Course, 1979.**

> **"When the background is complete to any given point the next factor presented or encountered in the same line of information will be learned and retained without comment, repetition, or practice." Ed Snapp, Southwest Texas CCDE Graduate Course, 1977.**

References

5.1. Snapp, Edward A. Jr., P. T., Unpublished lecture recording disc 14. Made available by Ed's daughter, Susan Snapp.

5.2. Snapp, Edward A. Jr., P. T., Lecture notes, Pflugerville, Texas, 1979.

SYNOPSIS OF *BUILDING BETTER LEARNERS*

Ed Snapp, (1925-2006) was the physical therapist that developed an educational program in the 1960's. His educational program is based upon human development that he theorized was retained in the Genetic Code and genetically passed on to the next generation at the time of conception. He named his unprecedented educational protocol Chronologically Controlled Developmental Education, CCDE, and started teaching CCDE to educators in 1975.

It was not Snapp's intention to get into the field of education. However, because of the diligence in his work as a physical therapist he was able to gradually associate human abilities in movement to learning abilities. Likewise, he eventually associated human disabilities in movement to learning disabilities. He found that when disabilities in movement were improved that learning disabilities were diminished.

Snapp began to question when does learning begin and how does learning occur. He concluded that learning begins at conception and that learning is aligned to the same path as the development of the human Genetic Code.

A baby, who begins life as a single cell, even at that moment of being a single cell, has the necessary Genetic information to provide him with a chronologically controlled prenatal development. A prenatal baby is not taught anything; yet, his abilities develop and increase in number when his prenatal environment contributes to his development. A prenatal baby will, most likely, be born in a predictable length of time with predictable learned movement abilities.

Snapp developed a time-line of learned developmental movement abilities. He used this time-line to know the sequence of movement.

For example, if a child had a problem with walking, Snapp could check this time-line to see what movements were in the sequential background to walking and Snapp would then work, not with walking, but with the background movements of walking. When Snapp realized that sequentially all movement began prenatally he then realized that not only was the prenatal sequence of movement important but the environment in which the prenatal movement was initiated was important, too. Snapp further realized that by incorporating prenatal developmental movements in a chronologically and environmentally controlled setting, children improved academically as well as physically.

He could now use his time-line to match his sequence of developmental movements to associated learning abilities in an associated environment. He was discovering that physical disabilities and learning disabilities did not have to be life-long disabilities. He was making a difference in education and that word was spreading. He was asked, "Would you teach an education course to teachers?" He replied, "What do I know to teach them?"

Ed Snapp knew that children initially and accurately learn by being told information, not by being asked for information. He knew that if a child has at least 90% accuracy in his learning, then—and only then—with this BACKGROUND he is ready to advance. He knew that if a child is within his PERCEPTION range to hear, see, and/or sense information of a single fact, that from that single fact his ability to learn is unlimited. He knew that a child's attention to learning is best when he is alert, not when he is overcome with FATIGUE (Snapp was concerned with neurological fatigue, not with muscular fatigue). He knew that if there were better teaching methods there would be better learning abilities.

The Snapp approach is to build LEARNING ABILITIES in each child. His simultaneous presentations of developmental, physical, chronological, and environmental factors make up his unique educational approach to developing better learners.

Distinct educational qualities of CCDE include:

- Learning environment, such as: light-controlled, distraction-free room; initially no desk, table, chair, computer, pen or pencil for the child
- Size of reading material print, and distance at which reading is viewed
- Size of writing, writing instruments, and distance at which writing is produced
- Sizes of objects manipulated
- Moving from CONCRETE to ABSTRACT learning in all subject areas
- Proceeding from LARGE MOVEMENTS to FINE MOVEMENTS
- Progressing through the developmental sequence of movement—prenatal, natal, postnatal, Basic Crawl, Homolateral Crawl, Cross Pattern Crawl, to Creeping
- Frequent inclusion of prenatal, natal and/or postnatal movements
- All subjects start with recognition, then a single fact and build to more complex series of facts
- Eye-Hand Tracking (Vertical, Horizontal, and Square)
- Attainment of minimum of 90% accuracy before advancing

Snapp's approach is unique in associating *specific movements* with *specific areas* of academic abilities such as:

- Eye-Hand Tracking *associates with* comprehension, development of total concepts, understanding of details, recalling of information, and prediction of movement
- Movement of the shoulder *associates with* handwriting
- Ball Rolling *associates with* reading
- Writing basic strokes from **SNAPP** Cards *associates with* visual memory and spelling
- **SNAPP** Cards *associate with* dominance in the ability to make quick decisions
- Rhythm *associates with* ball handling
- Language *associates with* **SNAPP** Cards, reading, spelling, and math

- Crawling *associates with* endurance, strength, coordination, and correlation of right and left sides of the body, correlation of the upper extremities of the body with the lower extremities of the body, correlation of the right brain with the left brain, and far point vision
- Teaching in the dark, in the twilight, or in the bright light *associates with* the proper area of Snapp's time line and environment in which a particular activity is learned
- Creeping *associates with* binocular vision, correlation of right and left sides of the body, correlation of the upper extremities of the body with the lower extremities of the body, and correlation of the right brain with the left brain

Every activity included in this book is purposeful and meaningful so as to "build" upon the BACKGROUND, PERCEPTION AND FATIGUE LEVELS of a child. These three concepts are crucial and necessary for *Building Better Learners.*

CHAPTER REFERENCES

Introduction

I-1. Snapp, Edward A., Jr., P. T., Workshop materials beginning in 1975.

I-2. Snapp, Edward A., Jr., P.T., The Language of Life, Health, Rehabilitation, Unpublished paper, 1990 made available by Ed's daughter, Susan Snapp.

I-3. Schmidt, Darlene, Parent Handbook, unpublished paper presented to parents of students involved in CCDE program at Southwest Texas State University, San Marcos, Texas, 1983.

I-4. Small, Roxanne, P.T., *Building Babies Better, Developing a Solid Foundation for Your Child*, Trafford Publishing, Victoria, BC, Canada, 2005, pp. 5-6.

I-5. ibid, p. 15.

I-6. Snapp, Edward A., Jr., P.T., Chronologically Controlled Developmental Education, Unpublished paper, 1983, p. 18, made available by Ed's daughter, Susan Snapp.

I-7. Ward, Betty J., Maximum Available Desk-to-Eye Distance for Students in Grades One and Two, Unpublished doctoral dissertation, 1989, Texas Woman's University, Denton, Texas; Internet: Betty J. Ward, PhD.

I-8. Alff, Lucy, Developmental Education, unpublished paper prepared for classroom teachers, 1977, p. 1.

I-9. Snapp, Edward A., Jr., P. T., course materials beginning in June, 1975.

SNAPP Principles

1-1. Snapp, Edward A., Jr., P.T., Graduate Course/Workshop, Southwest Texas State University, San Marcos, Texas, July, 1977.

1-2. Snapp, Edward A., Jr., P.T., Texas Woman's University Graduate Course, Denton, Texas, June, 1975.

1-3. Snapp, Edward A., Jr., P.T., CCDE Course, Pflugerville, Texas, 1979.

1-4. Grimes, Pam, Notes from Ed Snapp on fatigue as reflected from class shorthand notes taken by Pam Grimes at a CCDE Course, Pflugerville, Texas 1979.

1-5. Snapp, Edward A., Jr., P.T., unpublished paper presented at Texas Woman's University Graduate Course, Denton, Texas, June, 1975.

Foundation of Movement

2-1. Boyd, Margie, *Different—The Boy Who Couldn't Write*, Rockcrest Press, Georgetown, Texas, 2008, p 101.

2-2. Snapp, Edward A., Jr., P.T., Developmental Learning, unpublished paper, 2002 made available by Ed's daughter, Susan Snapp.

2-3. Small, Roxanne, P. T., *Building Babies Better, Developing a Solid Foundation for Your Child*, Trafford Publishing, Victoria, BC, Canada, 2005, pp 49-51.

2-4. Snapp, Edward A., Jr., P. T., "Developmental Exercises", unpublished material, Copyright 2002, made available by Ed's daughter, Susan Snapp.

2-5. Images adapted by Lucy Alff, 1982; Dr. Darlene Schmidt, 2011.

2-6. Snapp, Edward A., Jr., P. T., lecture notes, Pflugerville, Texas, 1979.

2-7. Snapp, Edward A., Jr., P. T., "Chronologically Controlled Developmental Education" presentation to Texas Association for Children With Learning Disabilities (TACLD), Austin, Texas, 1977.

Visual Perception

3-1. Snapp, Edward A., Jr., P.T., Quote from Graduate Course held at TWU, 1975.

Chronology of Reading, Writing, and Spelling

4.1. *Dorland's Illustrated Medical Dictionary*, 24th Edition, p. 340, Pub: W. B. Saunders Company, Philadelphia and London, 1965.

4.2. Snapp, Edward A., Jr., P. T., Notes from Workshop at SWTSU, 1977.

4.3. Snapp, Edward A., Jr., P. T., Quote from Graduate Courses held at TWU (1975) and SWTSU (1977).

Chronology of Math

5.1. Snapp, Edward A. Jr., P. T., Unpublished lecture recording disc 14. Made available by Ed's daughter, Susan Snapp.

5.2. Snapp, Edward A. Jr., P. T., Lecture notes, Pflugerville, Texas, 1979.

GLOSSARY—CCDE DEFINITIONS

Abduction: A movement of the extremities away from the center or vertical midline of the body.

Adduction: A movement of the extremities toward the center or vertical midline of the body.

Average: A statistical term—sum total of scores divided by the number of scores.

Awareness: Perceiving the initial presence or absence of any specific sensory input.

Background: The chronological development of perceptions, sensations, reflexes, and movement patterns that precede and are essential for the task being learned.

Basic Crawl: See Crawling below.

Basic Developmental Exercise: Exercises that involve basic movement activities and sensations used in specific environments that enable the nervous system to scan itself and to reinforce or repair any error that may exist.

Basic Movements: Basic developmental movements include: flexion, adduction, inward rotation, extension, abduction, and outward rotation and their release. (See Developmental Movements below)

Binocular Vision: Using both eyes together to converge and focus on an object.

Central Vision: Center of the visual field; the area where our vision is most acute.

Cerebral Cortex: The highest and most sophisticated part of the nervous system. It works best when the lower parts of the nervous system are working well. For it to work well it is dependent upon information it receives from the lower parts of the nervous system.

Chronological Order: The sequential order of development of the Human Genetic Code.

Correlating Cells: Nerve cells that subjugate other cells.

Comprehension: Complete understanding of sensations or materials being presented as demonstrated by application in various situations.

Convergence: The coordinated inward movement of the two eyes toward fixation at the same point at a given distance within twenty feet.

Crawling: (Prone position) moving across a surface with the face, palm of hands, inner forearms, front of the trunk, inner legs, and inner side of feet maintaining contact with the crawling surface. The three crawling patterns, in developmental order are: Basic Crawl, Homolateral Crawl and Cross Pattern Crawl.

Basic Crawl: Motor activity done with the body flat on the floor (prone position). Both arms are extended above the head but in contact with the floor. The head faces the direction of the side that has the knee raised to give leverage to push the body forward.

Homolateral Crawl: Motor activity done flat on the floor (prone position) with one arm extended and the leg on the same side of the extended arm raised to give leverage to push the body forward. After the forward push the head is turned to the other side with the other arm extending and the leg on the same side as the extended arm is raised to give leverage to push the body forward.

Cross Pattern Crawl: Motor activity done flat on the floor (prone position). One arm extends and the leg on the opposite side is raised to give leverage to push the body forward. The head is turned to the side of the extended arm. After the forward push the head turns to the other side as the other arm is then extended and the leg on the opposite side is raised to give leverage to push the body forward.

Creeping: Moving across the surface on one's knees and open hands with front of lower leg and top of foot in contact with the surface. Creeping is done using only cross pattern movements of the limbs.

Cross Pattern Crawl: See Crawling above.

Deep Pressure: A technique that affects deep muscles and receptors that are located on the surface of the bones. The deep pressure technique, as practiced by Ed Snapp, applies pressure into the muscle tissue until the bone is felt.

Developmental Environment: A setting that is concerned with the temperature, light, sound, and other sensory conditions associated with the specific developmental activity.

Developmental Movements: Basic Movements of a chronological order used in specific environments that enable the nervous system to scan itself and fill in gaps or correct any error that may exist.

Flexion: contracted muscles moving into the fetal position.
Adduction: a movement of the extremities toward the center or vertical midline of the body.
Inward Rotation: limbs rotate about the long axis of the bone, toward the front vertical midline.
Release of Flexion: the relaxation of contracted muscles, returning to a neutral position.
Extension: after the release of flexion, two adjoining body parts move away from each other by straightening the joint, increasing the angle at the joint.

Abduction: a movement of the extremities away from the center or vertical midline of the body.

Outward Rotation: limbs rotate about the long axis, toward the back of the vertical midline.

Dimensions Concepts: A developmental scale developed by Ed Snapp that includes:
   a) pre-dimension: early first trimester sensory or positional information that is not sensed consciously.
   b) one-dimension (1D): recognition or awareness level.
   c) two-dimension (2D): ability to acknowledge any two qualities; linear, area, rhyming, order, comparison.
   d) three-dimension (3D): three or more factors; volume, depth, analysis, organization.
   e) four-dimension (4D): innovation, projection, imagination.
   f) five-dimension (5D): visionary.

Dobie Cleaning Pad: Scotch-Brite™ Dobie Cleaning Pad™: Brand name for a plastic scrubbing pad that has no sharp edges to its fibers.

Dominant: Portion of the brain that is associated with quick thinking, quick acting, aggressiveness, decisiveness, efficiency, and protection. In terms of movements, it is the side of the body genetically determined at conception to be the most efficient side.

Echoing: Repeating or imitating the words or actions of another.

Estimation: Ability to quantify the total number of objects in a group of like objects without the sequentially counting of each item.

Extension: After the release of flexion, movement away from the fetal position.

Eye-Hand Tracking: Activities designed to increase the ability to locate and maintain visual focus on the hand as a moving target.

Eye-hand tracking is associated with eye movements, reading, writing, spelling, eye-hand coordination, comprehension, attention to detail, the ability to anticipate movement patterns, and the ability to predict consequences.

Extremities:
> **Upper Extremities:** the arms from the shoulder to the tips of the fingers.
> **Lower Extremities:** the legs from the hip joint to the tips of the toes.

Fact Teaching: Presenting information on a straightforward recognition level.

Far Point Vision: Use of vision when the viewing distance is greater than arm's length. The distance between the object and the person determines far or near vision.

Fatigue: See Neurological Fatigue.

Fine Motor Control: A function of the cortex that requires the use of central vision and/or use of the fingertips. It chronologically follows a base of gross motor control.

Flashing Light: Developmental activities used at the recognition or awareness level to enhance visual motor control and understanding of contrast; involves controlled distance, controlled degree of illumination, and controlled length of times for illumination, and for darkness.

Focus (visual): To adjust one's eyes to a specific distance in order to clearly see a particular object.

Flexion: A bending forward of two adjoining body parts that move toward each other by bending the joint, decreasing the angle at the joint; available in the trunk, neck, and joints of the elbows, wrists, fingers, hips, knees, ankles, and toes.

Friction Rub: Surface skin rubbed with enough intensity to create warmth and sensation.

Full Extension: As the baby emerges from the birth canal, full extension of the neck, trunk, hips, upper and lower extremities is now possible for the first time.

Fusion: Both eyes looking at a single scene or object, without double vision.

Function: The role of the various body systems and their parts.

Genetic Code: The specific sequence of changes that all individuals have available to follow in development from conception to death.

Genetic Time Line: From conception to death, each portion of development is introduced, learned, understood, and used as the background for the next aspect of development without teaching or training.

Gross Motor Control: Ability to use the large muscles in a coordinated manner, commonly used in walking, running and controlling one's posture.

Homolateral Crawl: See Crawling above.

Individual Positions: Specific placement of body parts used for specific movements.

Inward Rotation: Limbs rotate about the long axis of the bone, toward the front vertical midline.

Light Stimulation: Use of various controlled flashing lights or constant illumination of a given light in a controlled environment.

Light Touch Sensation: A skin on skin technique used to stimulate skin surface by using an extremely light touch across the surface of the skin.

Midline: An imaginary line dividing areas into two equal parts: top and bottom, left and right, or front and back.

Near Point Vision: Any viewing distance within the length of the extended arms, requiring both convergence and focusing of the eyes.

Neonatal: Developmentally, a time period from birth through the first 6 months of life.

Neonatal Extension: The stretching out of the limbs, trunk, and neck that should be possible during and after the time of birth.

Neurological Fatigue: When the nervous system can no longer maintain its attention to the activity at hand and process the information presented. After a period of correct responses, errors begin to occur and the desired learning can no longer take place.

Normal: A misused term. "Fully developed" would be a better term. An attainment of one's full potential.

Outward Rotation: Limbs rotate about the long axis of the bone, toward the back of the vertical midline.

Perception: The ability to be aware of and to understand sensory input and the brain's interpretation of that input.

Peripheral Vision: The outer ranges of the visual system that specialize in movement control, motion detection and position of objects in the environment relative to the side of the viewer.

Prenatal: Time period from conception to birth.

Prenatal Extension: As the legs and ankles extend and push against the uterine wall, the neck and truck flex; as the neck and trunk extend and push against the uterine wall, the knees and ankles flex.

Prenatal Light Touch: Originates with the movement of the amniotic fluid across the skin surface of the fetus and movement of the limbs against themselves and against the trunk to release flexion, adduction, and inward rotation. Snapp likens this sensation to the movement of a feather lightly touching the skin surface. Prenatal Light Touch can be done after birth to accomplish release of flexion, adduction, and inward rotation.

Prenatal Release: A mechanism that elicits a release from flexion, adduction, inward rotation to allow prenatal extension, prenatal abduction, and prenatal outward rotation.

Prenatal Sound: Auditory input to the unborn infant from and through the mother's body. In addition, recordings of the sounds available to the unborn infant can be purchased.

Recognition: Perceiving sensory input; an awareness.

Reversal: Mirror image, rotation, or improper order of letters or numbers.
Some examples:

b instead of d	m instead of w	p instead of q
h instead of y	p instead of b	u instead of n

saw instead of was
a single numeral written backward
31 instead of 13
314 instead of 413, etc.

Rough Skin Stimulation: Briskly rubbing a Dobie™ (scrub) pad or washcloth to create strong sensory input on the surface of the body that will aid the body in crawling.

Silhouette: An object's outline solidly filled in with black.

Slick Surface: A smooth area without indentations, raised spots or rough areas. This surface creates little to no resistance as one moves his body or body parts across it, allowing movement with as little friction as possible.

SNAPP Cards: White cards that contain black images, silhouettes, colors or written material on one side and white on the back side. The **SNAPP** Card is held in a stationary position with the image on the card facing away from the child, and rapidly "**SNAPP**ed" for less than 1/10 second by rotating the card as if on a horizontal axis in the middle of its height, creating the Thaumatrope illusion.

Subdominant: The portion of the brain that is associated with emotions, color, curves, sequences, ideas, thoughtful speech, humor, creativity, repetition, rhythm, story telling, and imagination. In terms of movements, it is the side of the body that is not the leading side.

Subdued Lighting: Another term for very dim lighting.

Total Body Extension: Occurs only after birth because the baby's environment has changed. There is no uterine wall to limit extension; the trunk, neck, and all limbs are able to fully extend.

Totally Developed: Correct use of movement, sensations, and perceptions.

Trimesters: Division of the total human gestation period of 40 weeks into 3 month segments; 1st trimester; 2nd trimester; and 3rd trimester.

Visual Memory: Recall of that which has been previously visually seen.

APPENDIX A: SNAPP'S DIMENSIONS

Ed Snapp used the term "Dimension" in describing functional levels of physical and intellectual abilities as well as describing the matching prenatal or postnatal environments. He used this term because "dimension" refers to position in space (the child's position in the matching environment) and time (the chronological sequence of child's development according to our genetic code).

When the unborn child has prenatal movements he cannot move across space; thus this is One Dimension (1D). When the newborn infant is in limited light on a flat surface, he has neonatal startle extension and rotational sequencing of arms and legs, but still does not yet have the ability to move across space. So the child's relationship to space still has only One Dimension. The 1D environment and 1D movements enable the child to learn about his own movement abilities without sensory inputs of other dimensions. Sensory cells, motor cells, correlating cells, and all other cells developing during this 1D time period are associated with each other.

The Two Dimension (2D) environment is more illuminated; this enables the child to connect his vision to his hand. Because he is flat on his stomach, with the side of his face on the surface, he uses the vision of only one eye. His vision of the left eye associates with the movement of his left hand and the vision of his right eye associates with the movement of his right hand. To move across 2D space the child is flat on his stomach crawling, using his monocular vision, palms or palm, palm side of his forearms or forearm, and the inner surfaces of his foot, knee and on a single leg. The child has the 2D relationship to the environment because of his movement across a flat surface. His success at moving in 2D is dependent upon the subjugation of 1D movement abilities. Abilities that are "subjugated" can be used automatically, without having to consciously be aware of or think about how the movement is to be done. Correlating cells developed during this 2D time period associate 2D with 1D and/or just associate with 2D.

Three Dimension (3D) illumination of his environment introduces the light (artificial or natural) and darkness that he will experience the rest of his life. The child is working in 3D when he moves across the surface in Cross Pattern Crawling. It is the cross pattern that makes this mobility pattern a 3D activity. He is also in 3D when he is up on his hands and knees rocking back and forth. He learns to use both eyes at the same time to look at his hands. He can then use his 3D vision to see where he wants to go while Creeping on his hands and knees. Snapp stated that according to the genetic code Creeping is always done using cross pattern movement of the arms and legs. Correlating cells developed during this 3D time period associate 3D with 1D, 3D with 1D and 2D, 3D with 2D and/or just associate with 3D.

Later the child will use his 3D vision with his use of opposing arm and leg movements to see where he wants to go while walking, running, skipping, marching, and/or using other combinations of movements that move him through space.

Snapp also used the term "Dimension" to distinguish ranges of intellectual functioning. One Dimension applies to instant recognition or awareness of single sensory input. An example is: perceiving a single visual input as a gestalt, with no analysis of what the parts or attributes of the object are perceived.

One Dimension is limited to being aware of the presence of a sensory input, such as being aware that a gong is striking, but no conscious awareness of the fact that it is a repeated sound of the gong, or being aware that the sound of the gong is now absent. In the case of the **SNAPP**ed cards, it is the instantaneous perception of the visual input as a gestalt—perceiving it in its entirety with no conscious awareness of any of the details on the card. A far point viewing distance is required for viewing the card in order to have it be a 1D function because closer viewing distance requires convergence of the eyes (3D). It is being aware of the prenatal light touch, aware of the surface on which the body is lying, of the presence of darkness (or an absence of illumination), or of illumination of the environment, of being aware of the surface and its quality(s); or being aware that something is new to him. One Dimension is just recognition, the simplest learning function. When recognition is all that is required, it is still 1D, regardless of the academic level of any information being presented. Learning of new material, regardless of the academic level, should begin in the 1D category and build from the student's 1D BACKGROUND.

Two Dimension applies to functions that may start at one point and move in one direction, such as deep pressure; or movement through space going in only one direction such as eye-hand tracking or hand movements to make large, wide strokes. Other 2D functions include comparison factors such as size or color when used to indicate a size or color, reading, certain ways of presenting spelling, counting, addition, subtraction, nursery rhymes, stories, singing, repetition, and sequencing.

Three Dimension applies to physical functions associated with the control of moving objects closer to or away from the eyes by bending or straightening an elbow, use of palm and fingers for holding a pencil, crayon or paintbrush, writing, coloring, cutting with scissors, convergence of vision, contraction of the pupils, and bouncing a ball. Additional 3D functions include answering questions, simple logic, awareness of details, and syllable phonics (the word is divided into syllables, with no analysis of sounds within the syllable: each syllable is recognized as a gestalt).

Four Dimension and Five Dimension employ use of the child's thoughts, which can move him through different levels of thinking; analytical thinking, projection of thoughts asking "What if" and projecting possible outcomes based on facts and logic. *Building Better Learners* does not go beyond 3D because the first three dimensions are developmentally appropriate for the chronological ages for which this book is written.

There is a given sequence of developmental activities in each Dimension. It was Snapp's intention for all 1D activities in all subject areas to be completed at 90% accuracy or greater before any 2D activities in any subject area were to be started. This intent would keep the 1D brain areas developing without interferences of the higher levels of 2D functions and 3D functions that stop 1D development when 1D development is not yet completed. Likewise, this intent would keep the 2D brain areas developing without interferences of the higher level 3D functions that stop 2D development when 2D development is not yet completed.

However, we understand that the contents within *Building Better Learners* could be overwhelming to newcomers. We also understand that every family's situation is unique and that your situation may seem to be more suited to moving your child through 1D, 2D, or even 3D activities in one subject area before you and your child work on another subject area, or even before your child has completed 90% accuracy in 1D activities of another subject. So, depending on your situation, your child could be working just on one subject area at a time or your child could be working at a 2D or 3D level in one subject area while continuing the developmental background at the 1D level in another subject. The best situation in terms of replicating the original learning process, according to the genetic code, is to be learning all 1D material, then learning 2D material, and then learning all 3D material. Doing so enables learning without gaps in the correlating connections. Complete learning of 1D, 2D, and 3D becomes the BACKGROUND for additional future learning.

At any given time any 1D activity may be recycled. Similarly, if a child is working in 3D activities, a 1D or a 2D activity may be recycled at any given time. The recycling of any developmental activity, at any given time, always serves to reinforce a child's abilities. To skip any 1D activity in this book is to skip development of those connections that provide for continuous learning from a lower level brain function to a higher level brain function.

APPENDIX B: SNAPP CARDS

Making the Cards

Make cards out of white 22" x 28" poster board, tag board, or card stock material. Poster board is recommended because the permanent ink of markers will not bleed through to the backside of the card. Inkblots on the back of the card will be distracting to anyone reading the card. Thicker cards work the best because they do not wobble when **SNAPP**ed. Folded or cut in half (longwise) copy paper, held against a stiff backing may also be used. The backside of the card should be of the same material as the front side of the card.

The length and height of the card is dependent on the silhouette, symbol, or number of letters in the word. A **minimum** card size for words should be four inches by eleven inches (4" x 11"). The completed Silhouette Card will be larger. The silhouette, symbol, or word should be placed in the middle of the card, centered top to bottom and side-to-side, leaving room at the sides to hold the card with the fingers and thumb. Use permanent ink when drawing on poster board. Water based markers will smear with the slightest contact with moisture.

1. Silhouette Cards (1D)
The Silhouette Card consists of a white card that provides the background for a centered black silhouette, one silhouette to a card. A black silhouette on a white card makes the best contrast. Silhouette Cards may be a different size, like 5" x 8" or larger, to accommodate tall silhouettes. Be sure all Silhouette Cards are the same size for ease in holding and **SNAPP**ing the cards. It may not be necessary to use a great number of silhouettes. Fifteen to twenty Silhouette Cards may be sufficient to help the child make the transition from concrete objects to representative "words".

Two examples of Silhouette Cards

"Cup"   "Tree"

2. Color Cards (1D)

Use matte finished construction paper or non-fading colored paper cut to fit the **SNAPP** Card. Completely cover the card, no white border. Glue the color to the front of the **SNAPP** Card. The back of the card should be white. The dimension of these Color Cards may be four inches by eleven inches (4" x 11") or larger.

3. Basic Stroke Cards (2D)

Each Basic Stroke Card contains a design that is one of nine strokes used to form written letters. The Basic Stroke Cards are a minimum of four inches by eleven inches (4" x 11") made out of white poster board. The design is made of a black line, a minimum ½" wide; one-inch wide would be better for some children. The length of the stroke should be short enough to leave a one-inch margin on all sides. Initially there is one basic stroke per card. Additional Basic Stroke Cards will be needed, some with two basic strokes, some with three basic strokes. Eventually Basic Stroke Cards with up to seven strokes per card will be necessary.

Present the following basic symbol cards in this order:

a) Vertical Line

b) Horizontal Line

c) Circle

d) Arcs
    (1) Top Arc

    (2) Arc Opening Right

    (3) Arc Opening Left

(4) Bottom Arc

e) Diagonal Line Starting Top Right

f) Diagonal Line Starting Top Left

4. Large Tracing Cards (2D)

Large Tracing Cards are not **SNAPP**ed, but are placed on the floor in front of the child. The child traces the design with the flat palm of each hand. The fingers of the flattened hand are straight and lifted from the surface so that more sensation is concentrated on the palm of the hand.

Each Tracing Card contains a basic design that is one of nine basic strokes used to form written letters or movements in drawing. The Tracing Cards are fourteen inches by fourteen inches (14" x 14") made out of white poster board and may be laminated to protect from dirt and use. The design is made of a 2" wide black stroke, at least 12" long. There is to be only one basic stroke per card.

Examples of Large Tracing Cards

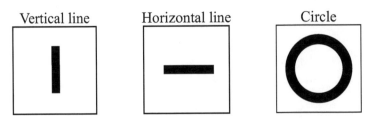

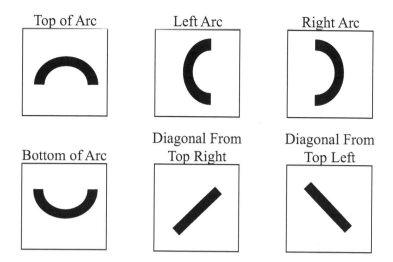

Top of Arc

Left Arc

Right Arc

Bottom of Arc

Diagonal From Top Right

Diagonal From Top Left

5. **SNAPP** Word Cards (1D)

As a general rule, the **SNAPP** Cards should have strokes that are a minimum of one-quarter inch (¼") wide. When making word or pre-writing cards the width of the stroke is to remain constant for the entire letter. If the viewing distance is greater than 8 feet, larger and wider strokes are necessary to make the letters or strokes larger.

When intended for viewing at an 8-foot distance, most letters are about one inch (1") wide, depending on the size of the card and the distance from which the child is reading the **SNAPP**ed Card.

Short letters (a, m, e, for example) should be about one and one-half inches (1½") tall. The tall letters (d, h, l, for example) and tailed letters (g, p, y, for example) should be about three inches (3") tall. Thus tall letters are twice as tall as they are wide. This width and height of letters is a good size for most children. When creating larger size word cards the ratio of height to width should remain the same: 2/1.

If the child is still having problems seeing the strokes, make the card larger and the strokes both wider and taller. It may also be necessary to create a greater distance than the minimum viewing distance of eight feet between the child and the card. Some children have required a distance as great as thirty feet to see and respond to **SNAPP** Cards.

If larger cards are needed, poster board can easily be used to make five and one-half by fourteen (5½" x 14") inch cards. These cards have enough space to easily accommodate larger sized words or larger sized dots.

Examples of homemade cards

6. Computer-made Cards (1D)

To make **SNAPP** Cards on the computer, print one word per sheet of paper, or print two words on a sheet and cut the paper in half. Use a landscape layout to make a **SNAPP** Word Card four and one-fourth inch by 11 inches (4¼" x 11"). Use a font that will produce the manuscript "a" (a child writes it by drawing a circle and short stick) and "g" (a child writes it by drawing a circle and a swing under tail). Although there are various styles for writing the manuscript letters "a" and "g", this style usually matches the style that is taught in handwriting textbooks. Often this font style is used in pre-primer readers. Snapp emphasized the need to have all parts of letters strokes to be the same width. Be sure to check out this aspect of the font you elect to use.

The following fonts will produce the manuscript "a" and "g" as suggested above to make the cards.

212

Tw Cen Mt Condensed Extra Bold (PC only)
Century Gothic (Mac) or (PC)
Century Gothic, when made bold print, comes nearer to having the strokes the same width for all parts of a letter.

The word is printed in black ink on white paper for the best contrast. Print the word, and then wrap the white paper around a piece of tag board cut to a size of four and one-fourth inches by eleven inches (4¼" by 11"). The shape can be modified for the symbol/letter/word size. An alternate way is to cut the paper the same size as the tag board then glue it to tag board, or it may be held against a stiff backing with the same sized white paper covering the back side.

If a child has a difficult time distinguishing the difference between tall letters and short letters, an extension can be glued on or drawn on the tall or tailed letters.

As viewing distance is increased, the width of the strokes and the size of the letters also need to be increased.

Examples of computer made cards

One-word Card

car

Two-word Card

the box

SNAPPing the Cards

The following is the procedure for presenting all the **SNAPP** Cards to the child. When the child sees the **SNAPP**ed card, he immediately names, reads, writes, or draws what he has seen, according to what he is instructed to do in response to viewing the **SNAPP**ed card.

The front of the card has the symbol or word to be read while the back of the card is completely covered with the same white that is on the front of the card. In preparation for being **SNAPP**ed, the card with the symbol or word is held in an upside down position as viewed by the adult, so that when the card is **SNAPP**ed the writing is in an upright position for the child to read.

In order to rotate the card quickly it must initially be held in a position where the child cannot see the front of the card. The **SNAPP** Card is **SNAPP**ed so quickly that the exposure time is less than a tenth of a second. This is in contrast to the usual so-called "flash cards" which have a much, much, much longer exposure time. The rapid **SNAPP**ing of the card on its horizontal center creates the Thaumatrope illusion, which gives the visual appearance of the image being suspended in space for a longer exposure. Rapid **SNAPP**ing of the card allows for instantaneous rapid recognition of the entire word and a rapid response to the word—as demonstrated by good readers.

The adult grips the midpoint of the ends of the card with thumbs and index fingers. The adult holds the card with the symbol or word rotated so that it is not visible to the child.

The Ready Position

Front View   Side View

Watch the child's eyes carefully. When he is looking at the card, say "When you see this, say _____", or in the case of writing, "When you see this, make yours like mine." When his response is to be verbal, tell him what the silhouette, symbol or word is, then rotate the card as quickly as possible so the silhouette, symbol or word is momentarily visible to the child.

The child should say the word immediately in a loud and positive voice or, in the case of written responses, immediately write on his paper the written symbol presented. If the child seems to have difficulty centering his eyes on the card, darken the room and have a light source from behind the child focused on the card: This gives a "movie screen" effect.

When two or more **SNAPP** Cards are held at the same time by the adult, **SNAPP** the stack and then move the front card just **SNAPP**ed to the back of the stack. Only the top card is exposed as the cards are **SNAPP**ed. **SNAPP**ing several cards together can only happen if all cards are made the same size. Some may find it easier to hold only one card for **SNAPP**ing, keeping the other cards face done in a stack at your side. Remember to handle the cards in a manner that does not allow the child to see the front of the card until it is **SNAPP**ed.

The adult's forearms must remain in a stationary position with elbows in a comfortable position out to the side. This stationary position makes the **SNAPP**ed symbols remain steady and motionless in space. If the forearms are moved during the **SNAPP**, the symbol's image is stretched and blurred. It is suggested that the adult practice in front of a mirror to verify that the image is not moving but appears to remain stationary.

The card is **SNAPP**ed as quickly as possible

At the end of the **SNAPP**, the child sees the white back of the card because the front of the card with the symbol or word is now angled toward the floor. At this angle the child cannot see the symbol or word on the front. After each **SNAPP** the adult can readjust the fingers and place the cards in a "ready position" for the next **SNAPP**. When introducing a new symbol or word, repeat the process several times. Expect and require the correct response. Never comment to the child whether he is right or wrong in his response. If he is correct, go on to the next card or the next activity. If he is wrong, set the card aside and present it again later as a new card.

If the response is not given quickly and correctly, set that card aside to be re-taught at another time. If he consistently makes errors or the responses are not made rapidly, he is not yet perceptually ready for this activity or he is fatigued.

Reading the SNAPPed Card

The child sits cross-legged on the floor in front of the adult at a distance of at least eight feet. This distance enables the child who lacks sufficient convergence to correctly perceive the card. The adult can sit on a stool or chair or stand in front of the child so long as the cards are **SNAPP**ed so that the child must look upward to see the **SNAPP**ed card. The child's abilities to comprehend and to recall are continually enhanced when information reaches his upper field of vision. A quick dominant response from the child reinforces his ability to react quickly and decisively with confidence.

Prior to the **SNAPP**ing of the card, instruct the child as to how he should respond to the card. The instructions will be different for each of the subject areas.

For example, in reading, say to the child, "When you see this word (cup for example), say, 'Cup'." **SNAPP** the card! The child says, "Cup."

In writing, say to the child, "When you see this (a basic stroke), make yours like mine." **SNAPP** the card! The child immediately writes the stroke without consciously thinking about it.

In Math, say to the child, "When you see this say (whatever the required response is)." Remember that the same card may have a different response depending upon the developmental stage you are presenting in Math.

Once several symbols, vocabulary words or Math concepts are learned, mix up the cards. Tell the child you are going to mix the cards within the different groups. Then tell him how he is to respond for that card. His response will indicate his accuracy of what he can do.

Require 90% correct responses before going on to additional cards.

APPENDIX C: DEEP PRESSURE

Snapp's Illustration of Pressure Points

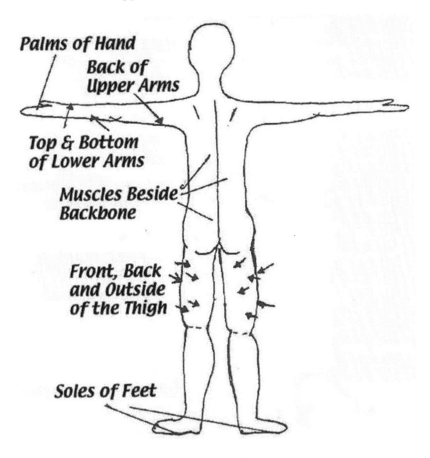

Points for Deep Pressure

APPENDIX D: SNAPP WRITING INSTRUMENT

Materials Needed

A. The Writing Instrument

1. One-half (½") inch thick marine plywood four inches by four inches (4" x 4")
2. One four inches by four inches by ½ inch (4" x 4" x ½") fine-pored sponge
3. One two inches (2") or two and one-half (2½") inches solid rubber ball small enough for the child's finger tips to be below the largest part of the cut-off ball, but large enough for the thumb and fingers not to touch each other, or for the fingers not to touch the board
4. One aluminum screw two inches (2") or two and one-half inches (2½") long
5. One aluminum washer as appropriate for the size of the screw
6. Waterproof adhesive that will bond wood, porous rubber, and the sponge
7. Knife to bevel the edges of the square piece of plywood
8. Scissors to bevel the edges of the sponge
9. Fine sand paper

B. Other Equipment Required

1. One six (6") inch aluminum pie pan
2. Black liquid tempera paint (or a very dark green or navy blue)
3. Liquid dishwashing detergent or liquid soap
4. Adult size short sleeve shirt large enough to cover the child's clothing: The buttoned shirt is worn backwards

219

5. A damp cloth to erase the writing surface after each pattern or a stack of empty paper if paper is used
6. A flat white writing surface or paper

Instructions for Construction

A. The Instrument

1. Bevel the edges of the plywood square from bottom to top so that the bottom of the square is larger than the top of the square.
2. Round the corners of the plywood square.
3. Sand all surfaces of the plywood square until smooth (no splinters).
4. Bevel the edges of the sponge from top to bottom so that the top of the sponge fits the bottom of the plywood square and the bottom area is smaller than the top area.

Writing Instrument: Side View from the Bottom

5. Cut off the bottom of the ball to a flat diameter of approximately one (1") inch, leaving more than half of the ball to be used. The ball should be small enough to fit in the palm of the child's hand and large enough that the fingers do not touch the plywood base. In making the writing

220

instrument the cut-off ball should be small enough to have the ends of the thumb and fingers below the largest part of the ball. The ball should also be large enough to not allow the thumb to touch the fingers and to not have the thumb or fingers against the board. You may need to try different size balls to find the best fit for the child. As the child grows, you may need to use a larger size ball.

Writing Instrument: Side View

6. Drill a hole through the center of the ball that is centered in the flattened surface of the ball and exits at the center of the opposite side of the ball. The size of the hole should be the same size as the shank of the screw.
7. Center the ball on the smaller side of the plywood square. Glue it in place and allow adhesive to dry or cure.
8. Place the washer on the hole at the center of the rounded top of the ball. Place the screw through the hole in the washer and through the ball, and screw it through the ball and into the center of the plywood. Screw tightly enough to have the washer and the head of the screw below the surface of the top of the ball. Be sure the screw penetrates into the plywood to hold the ball firmly in place.

Writing Instrument: Top View

9. Center the larger side of the sponge on the bottom of the plywood square. Glue it in place and allow glue to dry.

The writing instrument is now complete.

B. The Writing Liquid and its Container

1. Mix approximately one-half (½) teaspoon of liquid dishwashing detergent or liquid soap into one (1) cup of very dark liquid tempera paint. Mix thoroughly and store in a tightly capped container.
2. For a "writing session", pour approximately one-fourth (¼) cup of the mixture into the bottom of the pie pan. The depth of the writing liquid in the pan should be shallower than the sponge's thickness when the writing instrument is placed in the pan to load it with the writing liquid. This will allow the sponge to be loaded with the writing liquid without letting the liquid get on the plywood or the ball handle.

Child's Position for Writing

The child sits cross-legged on the floor with knees bent and with the writing surface centered in front of him. The pie pan with the writing liquid is on the floor next to the writing surface on the same side as the child's preferred hand.

To protect his clothing, the child wears a short-sleeved adult size shirt, with the buttons in the back.

Grasping and Loading the Instrument

To grasp the writing instrument, the child places his writing hand on the ball so that the entire palm is touching the ball. The fingers curve around the ball so that the bottom part of the ball is held by the entire inner surface of the fingers. This prevents using the fingers to make the required movements for writing, and results in using shoulder and elbow movements for forming the design, stroke, or letter. The guiding movements while using the writing instrument come from the shoulder.

The depth of the writing liquid in the pan should be less than the height of the sponge. To load the sponge with the writing liquid, the sponge side is placed flat in the pan holding the writing liquid.

To erase and clean the writing board after each stroke is complete, use a damp cloth. The damp cloth can be placed in a container with clean water to refresh and clean the cloth between erasures.

21284411R00148

Made in the USA
Lexington, KY
06 March 2013